Cultivating Connected Learning

CULTIVATING CONNECTED LEARNING

Library Programs for Youth

Megan E. Barrett
and Rebecca J. Ranallo

Foreword by Sari Feldman

Libraries Unlimited Professional Guides for
Young Adult Librarians Series
C. Allen Nichols and Mary Anne Nichols, Series Editors

LIBRARIES
UNLIMITED™
An Imprint of ABC-CLIO, LLC
Santa Barbara, California • Denver, Colorado

Library of Congress Cataloging in Publication Control Number: 2018003195 (print)

ISBN: 978-1-4408-5538-2 (paperback)
        978-1-4408-5539-9 (ebook)

22 21 20 19 18   1 2 3 4 5

This book is also available as an eBook.

Libraries Unlimited
An Imprint of ABC-CLIO, LLC

ABC-CLIO, LLC
130 Cremona Drive, P.O. Box 1911
Santa Barbara, California 93116–1911
www.abc-clio.com

This book is printed on acid-free paper (∞)

Manufactured in the United States of America

CONTENTS

Contents

SERIES FOREWORD

Hopefully you have the good fortune of serving groups of teens who love to hang out in your library. Library staff continually look for ways to keep teens interested in being there and provide them with opportunities to learn and create outside of the classroom, while expanding their peer relationships. Why not try connected learning? This approach allows teens to share ideas, to work with others, and to create and produce content, often using technology. The key to its success is that the topics are personally interesting to teens. This helps them achieve outcomes and sharpen skills outside of classroom learning.

Adding connected learning to your plan of service just got easier! Megan and Rebecca take you through the steps of how you can make this work in your library. Their knowledge on the topic is extensive, drawing upon their own library experiences with connected learning as well as research and practical advice. Using this book as a guide, you will clearly see that connected learning has a place in your library and how your teen patrons will benefit. It can also solidify your library's role in the community.

We are proud of our continued association with Libraries Unlimited/ ABC-CLIO, as they are committed to publishing practical quality works for library employees working with teens.

We hope you find this book, as well as our entire series, to be informative, providing you with valuable ideas as you serve teens, and that this work will further inspire you to do great things to make teens welcome in your library. If you have an idea for a title that could be added to our series, or would like to submit a book proposal, please e-mail us at bittner@abc-clio.com. We'd love to hear from you.

Mary Anne Nichols
C. Allen Nichols
Series Editors

FOREWORD

When Megan and Rebecca asked me to write the foreword to their book on connected learning, it gave me a pause to think about the ways in which learning models have evolved in library programming. Libraries have long been an environment that attracts youth during out-of-school time, but our role in supporting deep learning has changed over time.

Having started my career as a young adult services librarian, I know firsthand the challenges associated with providing positive and engaging experiences for youth. Today, librarians have to develop programming that not only engages youth but also addresses broader issues in substantive ways. Our work as librarians is driven by a need to move from outputs (i.e., number of kids coming to library programs) to outcomes (i.e., the library's contribution to improved high school graduation rates), making an impact on kids through meaningful library programs. This shift in thinking from outputs to outcomes has led to the application of 21st-century learning skills in library program design and a recognition that youth learn best when their learning is interest driven, peer supported, and academically oriented. Perhaps Benjamin Franklin saw this most clearly when he said, "Tell me and I forget, teach me and I may remember, involve me and I learn."

There is no question about the value of connected learning and the ways in which connected learning has transformed libraries. Libraries provide environments to experience new digital tools, to work collaboratively on projects, and to learn from staff and community experts. The library environment supports diverse learning styles and strengthens basic literacy as well as digital literacy through connected learning projects. As the opportunity gap widens, it is essential for libraries to create equity by delivering high quality learning experiences for all youth during out-of-school time.

In this text, Megan and Rebecca provide an essential guide for libraries and librarians ready to move to a connected learning environment and model of service. Beginning with the background information on the learning model and its benefits to teens, they continue the book with sections that detail the opportunities and options in connected learning programs. As libraries transform to be less about collections and transactions of service and more about focused learning opportunities, librarians would be well served to use this book as a timely and important guide for youth services.

The 2014 YALSA report The Future of Library Services for and with Teens: A Call to Action identified that "connected learning provides a foundation for what teens need and want from libraries. It reaffirms the value of libraries in the lives of teens." At the Cuyahoga County Public Library (CCPL), Megan and Rebecca have developed rich, outcomes-based connected learning programs that create learning experiences and opportunities for the teens in our communities. Their vision, experience, and knowledge come together in this book to stimulate our thinking about the ways in which connected learning can advance our profession and support powerful youth learning.

Sari Feldman
Executive Director, Cuyahoga County (Ohio) Public Library
President (2015–2016), American Library Association

PREFACE

Our connected learning journey began in 2014 with the creation of an action group of teen librarians from five branches of the Cuyahoga County Public Library (CCPL) system in suburban Cleveland, Ohio. Over the past three years, our five-location pilot has grown to include 20 of CCPL's branches. In this time, we have seen teens become engaged and explore their passions, sometimes traveling across the county to attend programs and access resources. We see less behavior issues in engaged youth and peer collaboration that is not forced. We have made connections with amazing volunteers and mentors who freely give so much of their time to a program that they believe in. It has been a pleasure to get to know them but also to see them grow and benefit from the work that they are doing. We have had the pleasure of working with staff to not only accept but really embrace this learning model. Our colleagues put their uncertainty aside to create programs that benefit their teens, functioning as facilitators and learning at the same time.

Connected learning is a method of programming in libraries that we truly believe in. We cannot promise you that your journey to implement a connected learning framework will be easy, but we can promise you that it will be worth the effort.

ACKNOWLEDGMENTS

We want to thank the many people whose contributions and support made this book possible.

To our colleagues at the Cuyahoga County Public Library (CCPL):

Our STEAMs, Jeanne Goldberg, Nan McIntyre, and Josanne Notaro, for the incredible amount of time and energy that you devoted to creating a STEAM volunteer program from scratch. We are forever indebted to you and appreciative of your hard work and dedication.

The cohort of CCPL teen librarians who have embraced the connected learning model and created original and impactful programs for our teens. You ran with connected learning when we asked you to and are true models of what teen librarians should strive to be.

Sari Feldman and Pam Jankowski for your support of the work that we are doing to make a difference in the lives of CCPL's teens. An extra thank you to Pam for understanding that this work means that there will always be a cart (or three) filled with both working and broken equipment outside of Megan's office.

And to our families and friends for your understanding and support throughout this experience:

Mom, Dad, Beth, Tim, Ed, Veronica, Timmy, Lilly, Mabel, and Gigi—MEB

Rob and Eleanor Bean—RJR

INTRODUCTION

CHALLENGES FACING TEENS

It may come as no surprise to hear there is a lack of equity in our current education system. Teens do not start out on a level playing field, and, unfortunately, they are not necessarily getting the skills needed to compete and thrive in today's world while they are in school (Ito et al. 2013, 14). An examination of recent research paints a concerning picture:

- Teens are not engaged in school.
- Crucial STEM skills are lacking.
- The digital divide still exists.
- The opportunity gap is widening.

Teens Are Not Engaged in School

Too many teens are disengaged and alienated from school. According to the 2016 Gallup Student Poll, 29 percent of students are not engaged in school and 22 percent of students are actively disengaged. Adding to this sad fact, disengagement only grows as teens progress in school. Not only are students becoming disengaged, but they are not hopeful for the future. The Gallup Student Poll also reported that 34 percent of students felt stuck and 19 percent of students felt discouraged (Gallup Inc. 2016). Without role models, youth are challenged to dream of their future. Teens who feel stuck struggle to see how they can move from their current situation to a future where they can succeed. At this young age, actively disengaging means that teens stop working toward building their future. They do not see their place in the educational system or the workforce and do not seek to build the skills that could engender future success. How can libraries combat these statistics and instill an enthusiasm for learning in these teens?

Teens' STEM Skills Are Falling Short

Recognizing that both technology and engineering are involved in many of the decisions people make daily, the National Assessment of Education Progress administered the first Technology and Engineering Literacy assessment in 2014. The assessment was administered to eighth-grade students to measure their knowledge across the following content areas:

- Technology and society
- Design and systems
- Information and communication technology

Less than half of the students (43%) performed at or above the proficient level overall (National Assessment of Educational Progress 2014). These critical engineering and technology skills are increasingly necessary to compete in a changing workforce. How can we create opportunities for teens to develop these skills?

The Digital Divide Still Exists

The digital divide is no longer just about people who have access and who lack access to the Internet. The issue has become more complex over time and now encompasses the quality of access. Many teens and their families are under-connected. According to the Joan Ganz Cooney Center at Sesame Workshop report *Opportunity for All? Technology and Learning in Lower-Income Families*, one in five families below the median income level have a mobile device as their only means to access the Internet (Rideout and Katz 2016, 39). Teens who do not have access to computers at home and teens who can only access the Internet through a mobile device are at a disadvantage to their peers.

In the journal article "A Library's Role in Digital Equity," Crystle Martin points out that "teens gain digital fluency through use of social media and digital technology. Young people who lack digital fluency will always be slightly behind their connected peers" (Martin 2016, 35). Comfort and fluency with technology is a pervasive issue. In 2016, the Pew Research Center reported that only 17 percent of adults are "digitally ready." The report defines digital readiness as comfort and confidence to effectively use technology (Horrigan 2016, 4). The bottom line is digital literacy is a necessity in today's world. From job applications to government assistance, people need to be able to connect to and deftly navigate websites in order to be a functional member of society. Digital literacy is no longer an optional skill.

The Opportunity Gap Is Widening

Teens spend almost 80 percent of their time outside of the classroom (Afterschool Alliance 2015, 3). These teens need to be engaged in something constructive, but many do not have the opportunity to participate in out-of-school time activities. While out-of-school spending has dramatically increased in wealthy families, spending in low- and moderate-income families has remained level. To put some numbers to this statement, higher-income families spent an average of $5,300 annually on out-of-school time activities for their children compared to the $480 spent annually by lower-income families (Afterschool Alliance 2015, 3). The widening opportunity gap is important because there is a strong link between youth who participate in consistent out-of-school activities and positive outcomes, including higher eventual wages, greater self-esteem, more civic engagement, and greater psychological resilience (Putman 2015, 174).

MAKING A CASE FOR CONNECTED LEARNING

Though all of these statistics may sound sobering, there are tested and true ways to make an impact with youth. Mentors and relationships with caring adults build engagement, hope, and connection to the greater world as a whole. Mentors help teens create connections to networks and resources. Study after study shows that youth that engage with mentors build hope for their future and reach for economic and social opportunities to succeed (The Mentoring Center 2017).

For the sake of future generations, we cannot continue on our current path. These statistics make this fact clear. As the economy shifts and as technology advances, the ability to adapt to meet changing and evolving needs is a requirement. However, while these statistics paint a grim picture, the outcome does not need to be so dire if we change how we view education and learning. Connected learning is well suited to address these critical issues. Embracing the connected learning framework can help counter some of these challenges. Connected learning recognizes that learning is a lifelong process that happens everywhere (Ito et al. 2013, 14). The framework moves beyond academic basics and makes learning relevant to today's digital world and workforce realities. So where and how do we start? Rest assured, we are not saying that a couple of library programs and some new pieces of equipment are going to solve all problems. What we are saying is that embracing our role as educators and working to create opportunities to connect young people with knowledge and resources can make a difference. We believe that combining libraries and connected learning creates environments where teens can be engaged and thrive.

HOW TO USE THIS BOOK

This book seeks to create a framework and path forward for libraries of all sizes to embrace connected learning. The book is divided in eight chapters that include the main areas that librarians and administrators will encounter when adopting connected learning. Each chapter contains background information to provide you with context on how the subject applies to connected learning, examples of how other libraries approach the topic, resources and tools to implement in your library, and action steps to help you begin. There are also additional resources, forms, and checklists in the Appendixes. The book does not need to be read in order—feel free to jump around based on the needs at your particular library or school.

Chapter Descriptions

Chapter 1—Connected Learning

This chapter provides information about connected learning, including the benefits of adopting the model and why libraries are a good fit for connected learning.

Chapter 2—Creating Your Plan

This chapter discusses how to assess your community's needs and tie your plan to the library's mission and strategic initiative. This chapter also includes information about funding, getting administrative and staff buy-in, and leveraging partnerships and collaborations for support.

Chapter 3—Finding Your Space

This chapter discusses how to create a space that encourages connected learning. This chapter includes lists of suggested technology and equipment, ideas about what to do when space is limited or even non-existent, and virtual environments.

Chapter 4—Developing Your Collection

This chapter discusses how to expand your collection development policy beyond the traditional library to include apps, online resources, and other equipment and technology.

Chapter 5—Staffing and Running the Program

This chapter discusses how staff mind-set may need to shift to fully embrace connected learning. It also provides information on why you should use volunteers and how you can create a volunteer program at your library.

Chapter 6—Planning the Programs

This chapter discusses how to develop and facilitate programs that support connected learning. This chapter provides you with ideas and resources to develop your own programs and several complete program plans to get you started in your own library.

Chapter 7—Marketing and Promoting the Program

This chapter discusses where and how to reach teens. This chapter also includes information about public-school library collaborations, collaboration with other community partners, and how to involve parents: creating buzz—the power of peers and word-of-mouth promotion, using the library website, blogs, and social media.

Chapter 8—Assess and Refine

This chapter discusses how to assess and evaluate connected learning at your library. This chapter also includes information on how to improve your program and how to prevent staff burnout.

Appendix A—Connected Learning Resources

This appendix includes links to a variety of online resources to support connected learning in your library. The resources have been divided into categories. Some examples of categories are funding and partnership resources, making and makerspace resources, professional development resources, and programming resources.

Appendix B—Forms

This appendix includes sample forms that you can use as tools to jump start your adoption of connected learning. Examples include a teen program survey, program design and cost worksheets, and a sample volunteer job description.

1

◇ ◇ ◇

CONNECTED LEARNING

Connected learning theory was first coined by Dr. Mizuko Ito and colleagues in 2012 as a participatory approach to youth learning through digital media and technology. The model builds on earlier research by Ito and her team, exploring the concept of teen learning through "hanging out, messing around, and geeking out," or HOMAGO. Connected learning takes HOMAGO further, detailing the type of learning that emerges from each stage of the concept and how deep learning can be achieved. Teens hanging out in the library are ripe for engagement. Messing around in a program can help define interests and build enthusiasm. Geeking out provides an opportunity to connect and develop a true passion for a topic.

YOUmedia at the Chicago Public Library, Chicago, Illinois

You simply cannot talk about connected learning in a library space without mentioning YOUmedia. The groundbreaking space at the Harold Washington Library Center in Chicago, Illinois, was the first of its kind to bring youth, digital media, and adult mentors together. Creation of the space actually predates connected learning but focused on the Hang Out, Mess Around, Geek Out (HOMAGO) theory from which connected learning grew. Both HOMAGO and connected learning emerged from research provided by Ito et al. (2010) of an ethnographic study featuring 700 youth. That research led to current thoughts about HOMAGO and connected learning engagement with youth. Inspired by the research, the Digital Youth Network partnered with staff at the Chicago Public Library to create a new model of youth engagement in libraries. The model of digital learning and inclusion was funded by the MacArthur and Pearson Foundations, among many others.

Opened in 2009, the first YOUmedia space was conceived to attract a diverse audience. The spaces at YOUmedia are creative, transformative, and dynamic spaces that put connected learning into action. They provide access to tools, technology, and people in an attempt to engage youth with digital media and each other. Incorporating the principles of HOMAGO means that YOUmedia has space for youth who desire to just hang out, as well as those who want to engage and mess around with tools. Youth who choose to discover their passions are truly geeking out in the space, finding opportunities to learn as much as they can about their tool of choice. The open nature and central, accessible location seek to promote equity and inclusion for youth who may feel disenfranchised in more traditional spaces. The openness of the space and the ability for youth to determine their level of engagement help increase the focus on youth interest and opting-in.

Adult staff and mentors are in place in the YOUmedia space to ensure that youth have clear pathways to enable the application of skills acquired in meaningful ways. Mentors not only support youth engaged in deep learning in project work but also provide ties to the application of that learning in the real world. Youth see the skills applied and in action in careers, giving weight to the impact.

The research was initially funded by grants from the MacArthur Foundation. MacArthur sought to learn more about how youth learn outside schools and the outcomes when youth dig deeply into their passions. Connected learning models engage learners with their interests, each other, and academics. They are equitable environments where youth are free to pursue interests without the limitations of a school district's resources. As schools moved more toward teaching to standardized tests, librarians began to realize the value of out-of-school time programming and connected learning environments when it came to interest-driven learning and their youth customers. Libraries present the perfect opportunity to engage youth with connected learning. They are hubs of access and engagement and have become, by desire and necessity, community centers that offer a safe place for individuals seeking belonging and support. In this chapter, you'll find some strategies to successfully integrate connected learning into your library environment and create a vibrant and sustainable program that grows with your staff and customers (Ito et al. 2013, 8).

Connected learning theory is based on the principle that learning happens in three spheres:

- It is interest driven.
- It is peer supported.
- It is academically oriented learning for teens.

These spheres can be separate and disconnected in a traditional classroom model but can find unity in spaces outside the classroom. The connected learning model builds upon the participatory culture in which today's teens have grown up to encourage engagement and mastery of learning through peer interaction and sharing. Connected learning focuses on the idea that everyone contributes and no single person is a master. All ideas have value and anyone can produce knowledge. In the same way, anyone can now be a content creator and contribute to the base of knowledge that is readily available for all to access. There is no requirement for formal training or education to produce content or knowledge; in fact, the act of working in peer groups to create new information and content is a form of education. Such a method engages the learner in productive collaboration and encourages information literacy and self-directed learning with the content of the individual's own role in group learning. Let us further explore the three spheres of connected learning and the shape that they take in libraries, starting with peer-supported and interest-driven (Subramaniam 2016, 2–3).

Connected learning is peer supported and takes the form of youth working together to create or produce content. Examples of content would be an animated video written, filmed, and edited by teens; a song that teens have written, performed, and produced; or a podcast that teens work together to research, write, and create. Other examples would be a chain-reaction machine built by teens or an art installation created and installed by teens. There is a shared purpose in youth working together in peer groups, with or without technology. Connected learning is about utilizing the participatory culture that today's teens have grown up in to harness a shared purpose and produce content or information. Teens are encouraged to openly network and share information and ideas to produce knowledge and content (cultural content). This can mean working together to create new content based on assessing information they find or curating existing content to produce something new. Either scenario creates a role for library staff to share expertise (Subramaniam 2016, 3).

Connected learning is a framework under constant development because it utilizes and depends on evolving methods of content creation and connection, often through technology. Though not essential to the process, technology adds ease of sharing, richness, and additional abilities to connect and disseminate the content that has been created. As technology continues to evolve and grow, so do the methods by which it may be utilized for connected learning in libraries. As youth grow and as access to technology becomes more ubiquitous, it is also more essential to connect learning environments. Mobile access is more prevalent among youth today, and libraries can draw upon the comfort that youth have in their ability to create content on their own devices to engage them in programming.

Aspects of connected learning hinge on producing content through remixing and curation using new media tools. Similar to the practice of sampling in hip-hop or rap music, remixing can involve utilizing a beat from a song, a pattern in a picture, or a line from a written work to create new content. This is technology available to anyone, and it crosses economic boundaries. Dramatic shifts in mobile and online technology that evolves quickly have led to the democratization of access and availability. Teens have access through multiple avenues and can often master the use of technology with little effort. Librarians are there as guides to assist in sifting through technology and resources, but not to restrict or control the process. They participate in the creation with youth, allowing them to take the lead. They are ideal partners in the assessment of information. Allowing youth to take the lead on content creation builds trust and respect (Subramaniam 2016, 2–3).

This can be an unfamiliar and uncomfortable position for some librarians; it requires release of their expert role and an understanding that they are abdicating control of the process. It does not mean that the programs are chaotic or out of control, but it does mean that library staff function as facilitators in the process, guiding students to the desired outcome. While this can feel disconcerting to staff who have spent their careers managing every aspect of programs and interactions, it is distinctly necessary for youth to engage in the peer-supported nature of connected learning.

Library staff who engage as facilitators also have the opportunity to learn in the process and that can be incredibly rewarding. Young people have much to teach, and librarians who function as co-learners engage more deeply. This can also be a solution for library staff anxious about the ever-evolving technology that is involved when utilizing new media tools. Youth are often quite adept at mastering these tools and it presents the perfect avenue for library staff to surrender control.

Connected learning spaces also focus on marginalized groups and equity of knowledge and access. Marginalized groups in communities are often less inclined to speak out and share interests and needs. Several decades of Pew studies have shown us that libraries are highly valued by marginalized groups and present a valuable opportunity to connect and encourage peer connections and learning. In many communities, libraries serve as a social connector, attracting many diverse constituents and offering the opportunity to form a connection to the community. This also presents an opportunity for marginalized youth to interact with a diverse audience and create connections with other youth in whom they may recognize similarities. Even if similarities may be unobservable, learners working together in peer groups create shared purposes. Connected learning promotes engagement across groups and differences by encouraging engagement around interests.

Studio NPL at Nashville Public Library, Nashville, Tennessee

In 2000, Nashville Public Library (NPL) opened its first dedicated teen space. They engaged a teen programming advisory group to recognize and channel teens' interests and topics. In 2012, the library system was awarded an Institute of Library and Museum Services grant to take their teen programming further with a space encouraging the next creative and innovative generation. Studio NPL is its connected learning space featuring a central studio at the main library and five other spaces across the system at the Green Hills, Bellevue, Southeast, Madison, and East branch libraries. Mobile equipment and programming ensure that the learning is not confined to just six branches within NPL's footprint. Mobile access means that any of NPL's branches can host a connected learning program to engage their community.

The spaces seek to encourage youth to create and contribute content rather than just consuming it. Founded on the principle that out-of-school time learning experiences are crucial to success in college and the workforce, Studio NPL seeks to provide youth with mentors and resources to learn digital literacy and valuable 21st-century skills. Youth have the opportunity to explore their passions and connect them to economic and academic opportunities. Nashville youth were engaged from the conception of the space, contributing ideas to the topics, equipment, and layout of the spaces.

Studio NPL spaces feature classes every afternoon, ranging in topic from audio and video production, spoken word, photography, 3D printing, electrical engineering, coding, animation, and more, depending on youth interests. There is computer access and audio and video equipment for project work and enjoyment. There is also a focus on graphic design for youth who seek immersion in the digital arts, including tools for digital imaging and design. Learning tools are left out in the open to encourage experimentation and self-facilitated learning (Nashville Public Library Foundation 2017).

Surveying youth interests allows marginalized youth to feel like they have a say and can make a difference. Listening to the responses of youth and programming to address interests help young people find a place in the library. Libraries have a long history of being centers of the community. Their role with marginalized groups has been established, making them an ideal partner in the connected learning realm. Libraries turn into hubs of connected learning for groups of diverse teens by truly engaging them in the topics and creation of programs. Surveying and teen advisory groups have worked well to engage teens and identify interests, but true connected learning happens when the teens themselves are included in the creation and design of programs geared toward them (Subramaniam 2016, 2).

It is give and take that makes connected learning work. Teens participate in program creation and design while working with adults and mentors. Both groups learn and engage in the process and build a bond that cannot be achieved through one-dimensional learning. Cross-generational learning between teens and librarians or mentors solidifies the value of teen ideas to the community. It reinforces to teens that they have something to contribute that is valid and valuable and creates more engaged members of the community. Embeddedness of librarians in this model is key to the trust of youth. It makes the librarians' role as curator of interests more efficient if they have gained trust and are a participant in the process with the youth that they engage.

Tying in the third sphere of the model, connected learning is academically oriented. Connected learning topics are tied in some way to the academic experience of youth. This can be directly in partnership with schools or through work on projects or subjects that relate to academic pursuits. In order for connected learning topics to have a deep impact, there has to be a connection to academic topics. This connection has an impact outside the wall of a library or a school, with the potential to direct the learner toward skills that can lead to economic and political investment and growth. Part of the learning evolves from the understanding that formal education is not the only option and that there are other methods that can be valued. New technologies can be harnessed to encourage learning over distraction. Unlike the physical world, which can be cruel, there is room for everyone in the digital world. Engagement with peer groups provides students the opportunity not only to connect over academic subjects but also to learn and make sense of learning on an individualized timeline. Technology can facilitate access to collection and networks of knowledge, and suddenly, peer groups can expand beyond physical geography. Learning can still be fun and fascinating while being directed toward achievement and excellence. Successes with peer groups can build the confidence necessary for youth to envision life-changing success and a different economic reality to work toward for their future (Subramaniam 2016, 3).

Homer Public Library, Homer, Alaska

You often read that it takes hearty stock to live in Alaska. Running a connected learning program in an Alaskan library is no different. The Homer Public Library is located in Homer, Alaska, southwest of Anchorage in the Kenai Peninsula Borough of the state. Homer is home to just over 5,000 people, and as you might expect, sometimes you have to get a little creative to make things work there. Fortunately for Homer, librarian Claudia Haines has a passion for engaged learning and all things digital. She is the accomplished author of *Becoming a Media*

Mentor: A Guide for Working with Children and Families, and she travels the country inspiring love for digital resources.

Librarians in small towns will likely understand that the challenge of a small town is that it is often only you making the efforts. Readers from the small town will also understand that the benefit of a small town is that you know your community, and engagement is a built-in part of what it takes to survive and succeed there. Such integration means that few community needs are hidden. Claudia recognized the need for engagement and started early with her community. She makes connections with families and youth at a younger age, integrating digital media and STEM activities into story times. As they grow, those youth can continue to engage with activities built to boost learning and self-sufficiency.

Regular programming throughout the school year ensures that youth are active participants in program structure and design. Claudia functions as mentor and facilitator but openly embraces the opportunity to learn along with youth in the community. Whether a community is large or small, the best way to engage is often to learn right beside youth. Other mentors have included high school juniors/seniors, community experts, and retired teachers.

Building topics in the connected learning model helps Claudia ensure that the library is leveling the playing field for all youth in Homer as much as possible. Homer Public Library is the resource available for out-of-school time learning. The library recently received a Libraries Ready to Code grant from Google and the American Library Association. The grant helps the library make an academic connection through its connected learning programming, adding a computer science and coding program that is not available through the local schools. It has also been an excellent opportunity for Claudia to engage local, high school–age mentors in the process, giving them the chance to increase their knowledge and learn valuable instruction skills (Haines, interview, 2017).

Ideally, connected learning environments support learners in effectively tying together their social relationships and networks with academic pursuits and individual interests. Engaging learners around their interests and encouraging peer connections is a first step, but relating youth interests back to academic topics is also essential to the model. Academic success is important to intellectual growth. Engaging youth with each other, their peers, and mentors is valuable, but going a step further and introducing relevant links to their academic lives is the final step in taking connected learning from community building to civic engagement and future economic opportunity. That is the value of connected learning: fostering an understanding that interests can strengthen and support academic pursuits, building future academic achievement and excellence. Demonstrating that there are many methods to link a learner's interests with academic pursuits can be life changing. Academic subjects and credentials become badges of achievement that demonstrate mastery of topics that learners value. This connection cannot be undervalued. It is the component that can lead to economic and political opportunity and true transformation.

The engaged and flexible nature of connected learning also builds 21st-century skills in connected learners. Learners who can shift their skill sets for the jobs and innovation of the future will be valued and in high demand.

The connected learning model is ideal for teen learning. Teens seek peer groups, belonging, and a sense of purpose. Participatory learning, when interest driven, can foster a sense of belonging and is well suited to youth who have grown up and developed in the current culture of knowledge sharing. They have grown up learning to curate and consume knowledge readily available online. When pairing collaboration among peer groups with participatory learning, teens can recognize the benefits of connecting with peers in close proximity and to the larger community as a whole through technology, fostering belonging both near and far.

Classroom and school-based learning are not always suited to the connected learning model. The structure and focus on teaching to a test can limit the formal school model's ability to allow the flexibility of connection and interest-driven content. Those models lend themselves to environments more conducive to connected learning principles, where youth are encouraged to work together to creatively seek solutions. Schools that embrace the maker movement or content creation may offer viable opportunities to engage youth in connected learning. The same applies to those that focus on problem-based learning or models that seek high collaboration and group problem-solving. Media specialists and schools working to incorporate connected learning in schools often point to the school library as the ideal fit for connected learning. School libraries function as a safe place for all learners. They are not tied to content in the same way that classrooms often are and provide a more flexible learning space. School librarians are already adept at guiding their students through the learning process on topics of their choosing, offering the academic space that supports individual learning.

Perry Meridian Middle School, Indianapolis, Indiana

Perry Meridian Middle School is just outside Indianapolis, Indiana, and serves a diverse economic student body with varying academic needs. Librarian, Leslie Preddy, author of *School Library Makerspaces: Grades 6–12*, has been a school media specialist since 1992 and is a strong advocate for makerspaces in school libraries. Preddy promotes connected learning principles throughout makerspace advocacy, noting the similar focus and outcomes. At her school library, Preddy works to build a sense of community and is often considered the go-to tech person. She argues that life is often "project based" and teaching these skills prepares students for the work world where perseverance is essential to success. The library's environment is welcoming to all students, and Preddy is already accustomed to assisting students seek out information on their individual interests. Her library is unencumbered by testing topics, and she can encourage creativity and innovation.

Interest-driven programming, hands-on tools, and digital media technology bring opportunities for distinct learning. The hands and mind are engaged together. The busy nature of a school media space ensures that students rely on problem-solving and peer groups for some of the work. At the same time, Preddy is there for support and builds strong bonds with students. The project nature of the work in Preddy's space requires students to finish tasks and work through problems to achieve their goal. This builds a different type of endurance and focus that youth have not always developed. Preddy also encourages collaboration with teachers to incorporate projects and learning goals into the classroom. She believes that this connection leads to deep learning that sticks with students.

The experience with making and connected learning at Perry Meridian Middle School has been a positive one. See, learn, and do is a perfect fit for a middle school library media center. Youth have embraced learning and making, collaborating with each other to accomplish their goals. Preddy is working now to support teachers at the school in incorporating more projects into their curriculum. For both teachers and students, she scaffolds pathfinder guides to structure thinking, but leaves plenty of room for exploration and problem-solving. Her goal is to guide youth in developing innovation skills and embracing failure as they become more resilient learners (MakerBridge 2017).

School libraries with makerspaces are already accomplishing connected learning work. These spaces help students dive deeply into topics of interest. The nature of learning with maker equipment and digital media equipment requires persistence and growing accustomed to making mistakes and persevering. Media specialists point to this process to endorse a making model similar to connected learning. Perseverance changes the mind-set of students and moves them beyond abandoning a project when it becomes tough. School media specialists are often busy doing multiple things in their spaces, requiring youth to rely on each other and become somewhat self-sufficient with equipment. The media specialist can drop in and problem-solve as needed, but the overall environment lends itself to peer groups and support. Finally, media specialists are in a unique position to connect with educators and work digital media into classroom curriculum where possible. This further extends connected learning into the academic sphere and draws the model into the classroom (Fontichiaro 2014, 1).

New Milford High School, New Milford, New Jersey

Laura Fleming, author of *Worlds of Making: Best Practices for Establishing a Makerspace in your School,* is the media specialist at New Milford High School and has been in the district for more than 20 years. The district has received publicity for incorporating its makerspace as a way to increase student engagement and connect interests to learning. Fleming mainly functions as the mentor but takes a very loosely directed approach to instruction. Her goal is to see where the students take their learning and to avoid putting too many constraints on the process. The makerspace includes a mixture of hands-on learning and technology, with a design that encourages youth to sit down and begin tinkering without teacher facilitation.

With a strong belief that "makerspaces are a part of a vibrant school library," Fleming utilized connected learning principles and ideas in the creation of the space, building support from the beginning. Integrating hands-on learning within the traditional library media center space allows Fleming to reach youth who may not have been engaged in the process before. Different methods of learning are strongly supported by connected learning methods where no judgment exists for how youth want to immerse themselves in a topic. In fact, such differences allow youth who have connected with peers to observe other opportunities and methods for learning. The diversity apparent in individual knowledge acquisition can benefit youth when facing future challenges and obstacles.

Fleming has ensured that her library's makerspace enhances classroom learning by doing her homework. "Before I ordered a single piece of equipment [for the makerspace], I did a thorough survey of students' existing interests," says Fleming. "I also looked for ways that the makerspace could supplement areas in the academic curriculum that were thin, or make available to all students activities that had previously been open to only a select group" (SLJ 2015).

The focus on the space was also a frugal one. Fleming is a strong believer that limited materials spark creativity and the limited budget forces students to become more innovative to accomplish their goals. Much of the technology in the space has been built by the students, including a computer created from littleBits housed in a 3D printed box. Other technology in the space includes stations for Legos, 3D printers, a littleBits bar, and take apart tech.

Fleming believes strongly that the experience has benefits for youth beyond the classroom and library. The act of creating and problem-solving sparks a deep interest that extends to career inspiration and future imaginings. She approaches projects and tasks in the space from a scaffolding standpoint, making some instruction available at the onset but gradually allowing youth to take responsibility for their own learning. Engaging peers with similar interests in problem-solving increases the potential for strengthening bonds and deep learning (Yorio 2016).

Implementing a connected learning model in schools can be hard to envision for teachers in schools in a similar way to librarians in libraries envisioning the model. The idea sounds great, but modifying curriculum to accommodate and putting it into practice can feel like an enormous step. The application of connected learning in schools revolves around flipping the learning model around and putting students in charge—not of the classroom management and not of the structures, defined or invisible, but of the topics and knowledge being pursued. Making students partners in the design of classroom learning builds engagement and trust the same way that including them in library program planning does (Mirra 2007, 1).

School-library partnerships are also possible alternatives, where libraries can offer a more flexible environment that complements the academic focus, but allows for more group work and content sharing. Both have an interest in preparing youth with 21st-century skills for a technology-rich future. Librarians have unique opportunities to motivate mentors and volunteers to engage young people and share expertise in a less formal environment. The opportunities for cross-learning and sharing of knowledge abound in this type of environment, and the added satisfaction for both mentor and youth is increased. This offers additional opportunities to tie interests and knowledge to real-world experience and possible career interests for youth. Mentors and volunteers are examples of interests in action and can help teens develop goals to work toward to attain experience and knowledge necessary for future pursuits.

North Royalton Schools and Cuyahoga County Public Library, North Royalton, Ohio

The Cuyahoga County Public Library embarked on the process of transforming the teen programming in all 27 locations into connected learning programs. The process started with five pilot branches that represented a diversity in community, school district resources, library branch space, and teen group composition. The five locations were specifically chosen based on staff interest and the diversity of need in their communities. They would eventually provide excellent models for the differing communities and spaces of Cuyahoga County Public Library's branches. Several of the five pilot branches had vibrant after-school teen attendance, and they sought to engage those populations with on-the-floor programming and regular activities. Several other branches had excellent attendance by teens at scheduled evening programs. Of the five pilot locations, it was the North Royalton branch that struggled to find the right time for an audience. The teen librarian, Shannon Sanek, was offering engaging programming in which her teen audience had expressed an interest, but they were often overscheduled and pulled in many directions. Shannon had already forged an excellent relationship with the North Royalton schools, specifically with media specialist Laura Whitehead. Laura and Shannon quickly developed a plan to offer Shannon's programming at the schools. Once a month, Shannon brings one of the library's iPad labs to the schools, and interested teens spend their lunch period in the school's media center working through a connected learning exercise. Examples of programs have included stop motion animation, Scratch digital animation, and coding. Laura's interest in the programs reinforced the connection to the academic aspects while encouraging students to continue learning even when Shannon was not there. Teens also sought Shannon out at her branch to continue the work they had started.

The successful partnership between the North Royalton branch and schools even led to some additional support from Cuyahoga County Public Library in the form of a $5,000 Innovation Grant. The grants were supported by the Cuyahoga County Public Library Foundation and were awarded to 10 branch staff who submitted proposals that demonstrated innovative ideas in programming. Shannon collaborated with Laura at the schools to develop a proposal for a collection of technology, things like Makey Makeys, Raspberry Pis, and Google Cardboard, to make available to teachers in the North Royalton schools. Laura lends out the technology and makes the connection to both connected learning and Shannon's programming at the library, increasing connected learning knowledge at the schools and teen attendance at the library.

Tying all of the pieces together, whether you are in a community library or school media center, you can reach teens with strong 21st-century skills and a desire to share them with their communities. The value of connecting interests with academic learning is great. Subjects that are personally interesting and relevant to teens foster higher learning outcomes. They encourage the learner to dig deeper into the topic and truly master it. Such topics are the ones that we as adults point back to and reminisce that we would have loved to work in a field that tackles those issues every day. Connected learners identify their interests and dig deeply while engaging peers with similar interests. Mastery of the topic builds confidence, self-esteem, and perseverance. Youth have access to technology or expertise not available elsewhere and a community with which to share it when they connect to each other, the larger community, and the world.

Add mentors to the model and you have a transformative combination. Mentors bring out the true impact of the learning and the real-world opportunities. Mentoring helps learners grow emotionally and create social connections. Youth engaged with mentors build communication skills and flourish in their ability to articulate their interests and projects. Mentored teens are more likely to avoid trouble and steer toward success. Libraries can be the key to all of this, doing what we do best by cultivating a network for youth in our communities (Rhodes 2017).

SUMMARY

Connected learning can be a powerful framework for teen engagement. Libraries that seek to forge a stronger bond with their teens and make a deeper impact can find a valuable resource in connected learning research and examples. Connected learning programs also present excellent opportunities for staff development and mentor engagement.

ACTION STEPS

1. Determine if your community could benefit.
2. Identify willing staff, partners, and organizations.
3. Consider intended outcomes.

2

◇ ◇ ◇

CREATING YOUR PLAN

Creating your plan before moving forward to generate support is essential. You may not have all of the details worked out, but an understanding of your community's need, your assets at the library, and the type of support you will need will help you convince your administration, your potential audience, and possible partners.

Start by evaluating your community. Seek statistics, reports, or data that show the needs. Things like the percentage of free lunches at your local schools, literacy levels, and high school and postsecondary attainment are all indicators of the level of poverty and advancement. Look at the economic health of your community and the level of entrepreneurship. Also look at how youth are supported and the prevalence of mentors. All of these factors can present openings for the benefits of a connected learning framework.

Questions for Evaluating Your Community

- What is the percentage of free lunches in your school district? This is a key determiner that shows the percentage of families living in poverty in your community.
- What are your community's literacy levels? This could include traditional literacy as well as digital and media. Are these levels rising or falling?

- What are the percentages of GED, high school graduation, and postsecondary attainment? Are they rising or falling? Are students seeking some sort of skills training, post high school, even if it is not a four-year degree? This will tell you something about local opportunities and whether teens feel that they can seek more from their future.
- Does your local school district have a STEM education program? Computer science program?
- Has the community lost industry or a major employer lately? Is it bouncing back with new opportunities for residents or viable retraining?
- Is there economic investment in the community?
- Are youth encouraged to dream and supported in pursuing dreams? This might not be a question with data, but it is one that is essential and talking to local teens can give a sense of the answer.
- Are there mentors prevalent in the community? Are there adults looking to encourage youth to engage in community and encourage them to learn more about topics in which they may be interested?

Some of these questions may be answerable with data and some with observation or conversations. All will help you start to construct a plan for a connected learning program that supports teens and addresses some of the needs in your community.

From your community scan, pick one or two areas that you might want to focus on. These can be the starting point of your connected learning program. They can be large or small goals, things like "I want to start an after-school drawing club," "I want to get funding for a couple of iPads to try some digital animation programs," or "I want to start a coding club." Focus on what seems attainable for your teens and your community right now and look at building toward more later.

Consider your goals for implementing connected learning, whether it is an extensive program or a single event. How will you reach your goals? How will you know when you have reached your goals? This is where outcomes come into your plan. Your outcomes are how you demonstrate that you are reaching your goals. Outcomes go beyond the typical outputs of things like attendance numbers and demonstrate the impact that a program is truly having. You can adjust outcomes as you craft a more detailed plan, but this is a great point to get a sense of the impact you truly wish to have.

Are you having trouble getting started? Does it all seem like too much to design a whole program and sell your administration before you have really tried it? Think about engaging in some backward design of the project. Backward design is the process of setting your goals for the project or program before deciding on all of the specific elements. The concept was originally introduced by Ralph Tyler in 1949 referring to the process of stating objectives. In 1989, Jay McTighe and Grant Wiggins applied the concept to curriculum and program development. By starting your process with determining the goals or outcomes that you hope to achieve, you can ensure that your learning activities lead you to your desired outcome because they will be constructed with that outcome in mind. This method also works well for projects that have multiple elements and responsibilities. After identifying the outcomes and methods to reach them, backward design allows you to assign responsibility for a whole project or specific pieces. This helps to clarify responsibilities that the project entails and to clearly communicate those responsibilities to the project team. Breaking down the process into specific elements allows you to tackle them one at a time without trying to determine everything at once. It also helps to ensure that all elements of the program or project are included, thought out, and assigned to someone. We provide a great chart in Appendix B that will help you walk through the backward design process. You can use this for the whole project, for every program you develop, or for both (Wikipedia 2017).

GENERATING SUPPORT

Libraries, by nature, have cautious cultures. Librarians are stewards of public funds, preserve information, and seek the right information/answers. None of those roles embraces quick decisions or spur-of-the-moment shifts in policy. Administrations require convincing that a shift in direction is beneficial and valuable. Different libraries and library systems have very different administrations. One system may have a progressive administration that openly seeks change. Another may have an administration that is rooted in the past and has a hard time with new approaches to traditional programming. Still others may require input from local government or school administration. Every form of administration presents its own challenges; the key to moving projects forward and generating support is to understand how your administration works and what will earn their support for change. Understanding some key aspects of how your administration works will serve you well when seeking to generate support for a shift to connected learning.

CONSIDER YOUR ORGANIZATION

Understand Your Mission

Know the mission of your organization. This may seem obvious, but being able to articulate how connected learning ties to your organization's mission and how it will benefit your library's customers immediately ensures that the idea is relevant to the organization. Knowing your library's mission and tying your endeavor to it will help your administration see the value of your project. It will also help you confirm that you are constructing a process that truly benefits your individual community.

Know Your Organizational Priorities

Before approaching administrators and stakeholders for their support, ask yourself these questions:

- Does your organization seek to promote and support youth engagement?
- Does it seek to engage teens in the community?
- Does it seek to promote an information-literate community?
- Is there a need to engage a large group of youth during after-school hours?

All of these needs and many more can be addressed with connected learning. The key is to know the priorities of your organization and to tie the benefits of connected learning to it.

Know the other pressing issues that affect your administration:

- Is there a budget shortfall?
- Are there security concerns?
- Do you anticipate trouble convincing the community of the library's value?
- Is there a new board of trustees or executive leadership?

Sometimes, that biggest challenge for a new project is timing. The more you can be aware of the pressing issues that affect your system, the better prepared you can be to ensure that you are proposing a change that is valuable at the present time. Understanding how the shift to connected learning may impact any pressing issues will only benefit your argument.

CONSIDER YOUR ADMINISTRATION

Know Your Personalities

What drives your administration? It will benefit your argument to know who in your administration has a passion for youth engagement.

Or know who views programming to engage seniors as an urgent need or who views the need to engage refugees or immigrants as essential. All of these topics and many more can be addressed with connected learning. Understanding the topics that your administration is passionate about will help you make connections that can generate support.

Know the Approach That Has Worked in the Past

An understanding of recent programs that have been initiated and how they were presented can help you develop an approach for presenting the value of connected learning that will elicit support. Looking at successful initiatives will also provide an opportunity to understand how your community responds to new programs and what it values. You can use past programs and initiatives to gauge whether your administration and board prefer lots of data, or if partnerships are the most convincing. It could be that they want to know about other libraries that are doing the same kind of work and the outcomes that they have seen. Or it could be that all of the above are necessary. Whatever the situation may be, looking at other programs that have gained their support should help you create a plan to convincingly present the value of your program.

Show the Value

Demonstrating the value of a proposed change is essential. Some of this should be apparent as you connect the idea to your mission, but any opportunity you have to demonstrate how connected learning can help your organization is beneficial. The community research you did will be useful here to demonstrate that you have sought to identify the needs of your community. It may seem like the value will be apparent in the connections that you make to mission and community needs, but it never hurts to spell out the value in detail. In fact, seizing the opportunity to demonstrate what is possible with current resources and make the case for what else is possible on a greater scale can be very effective. The outcomes and goals you have identified in creating your plan will help you focus the benefits you are seeking to achieve. Show how engaged youth can be. Show them the learning that can take place. Show how technology and collaboration can impact literacy. Pair seeing connected learning and engagement in action with describing the value and it is hard to deny the potential results.

Demonstrating Youth Engagement

For some, engaged teens are easy to spot. You know the buzz and feeling in a room full of teens who have made a program their own. There is a hum, and the teens have completely taken a project and run with it. To others, that room might seem loud and without a clear leader, but an engaged connected learning space is often quite energetic. Images, testimonials, or videos are great ways to demonstrate teen engagement to others. If the idea of a video seems intimidating, why not ask your teens to create it? You are their mentor, guiding them to portray the best of learning at the library; they are channeling their passion and enthusiasm into showing it their way.

Show the Cost

If you believe that you cannot execute a connected learning program with existing resources, make sure that is clear to your administration. It is worse to come back with an unexpected cost than to outline the cost up front. Even though any cost may be a deterrent for some libraries, transparency about possible costs will present you with the opportunity to offset it with the value. It will also ensure that your administration understands that you have considered all possibilities and methodologies when designing the program. Keep in mind, too, that you can always start out with a low budget program and build on it as your administration becomes sold on the idea. Connected learning programs do not have to be expensive ventures. There are plenty of low-cost options to pursue while you demonstrate the value of the programming to secure additional funds.

Keep Trying

Hopefully, your first attempt at convincing your administration will be a resounding success, but if it is not, keep trying. Look for new opportunities to promote connected learning as a solution to a new problem or seek out the new administration as they enter the organization. There is some finesse to understanding the difference between being annoying and being persistent, but the key is to continue to look for the right time to implement the program for the organization. Often, when you are ready to do something, the organization is not yet ready. The secret to success lies in understanding your organization well enough to make the suggestion at the correct time. Be open to partially implementing a program and building on it. Even a partial implementation can demonstrate the value and secure more generous support. Flexibility can help you achieve longer-term success.

Employing Emotional Intelligence

Emotional intelligence is considered a skill for managing and leading staff. While it has numerous applications in the management realm, it is also applicable when seeking to understand and work within your organization's goals and time-line. Applying the emotional intelligence principles of self-awareness, empathy, self-control, and emotional awareness allows you to recognize and account for your motivations and those of other staff in your organization. This can be very beneficial when approaching the elements of connected learning that require you to push yourself outside of your boundaries or when you are pushing other staff to do the same thing. In brief detail, the elements of emotional intelligence encompass the following:

- Self-awareness—knowing your own capabilities and limitations, receiving feedback, and self-reflection.
- Self-regulation—accepting emotions, understanding ways to control or man-age emotions, building trust and confidence in others.
- Motivation—knowing and understanding your own motivations.
- Empathy—understanding other's emotions, being able to relate; understand-ing other's emotions may not be the same as understanding your own.
- Social skills—managing the interactions with others, connecting, and listening.

To learn more about emotional intelligence, try starting with the following resource: Goleman, Daniel. "What Makes a Leader?" *Harvard Business Review*, November-December 1998.

CONSIDER YOUR STAFF

Convincing Staff of the Benefits of Connected Learning

Convincing your colleagues that change is good may be one of the hard-est things that you have to do. Libraries have existed and provided some basic services for a long time, and convincing some staff that change is beneficial is tough, especially when that change involves technology or pushing staff outside of their comfort zones. The reality is that many of your staff members are probably applying elements of connected learning already. Being able to recognize that elements of connected learning are present in current programs is beneficial to demonstrating a clear path from existing programs to a connected learning model. For much of the history of libraries, librarians were the experts who had an answer. Mov-ing from that role to a facilitator can be very uncomfortable for some staff. Understanding that discomfort and acknowledging it is key to helping staff push through it. Also key, though, is that just recognizing it is not enough or OK. Libraries stay relevant by evolving, especially with youth. It is not enough for staff to recognize their discomfort but remain stuck in the same position.

The process is long. Often, staff will make great strides at the outset but then slide back to their comfort zones. Teens are also a changing group of faces. Youth in libraries grow up and move on and continuing to engage each new group of teens and identify their interests is essential to keeping them engaged. We will not gloss over the fact that this presents additional challenges and work for staff. Reaching out to each new teen who comes into the library takes commitment. Also, connected learning facilitators are focusing more on engaging their teens and less on planning out every detail of every program. Embracing the role of facilitator means that staff will no longer be the expert but that they can find their place and become comfortable there. It also means that they will be forever learning along with their teens. This is often a personal journey for staff to figure out where they are most comfortable as a facilitator and learner.

Talking Points for Engaging Staff

Change is hard and asking staff to embrace change for your program can often seem insurmountable. Appealing to the changes that can directly benefit their work environment is one option. Appealing to their interests and own passions is another. Try the facts and ideas in this list as an approach.

- More engaged teens lead to fewer behavior problems.
- Teens are tackling problems or projects that will benefit our library.
- The partnership with the schools is bringing needed funding to our teen programs.
- The partnership with local business (or grant, etc.) is bringing the library equipment that we could never have been able to afford on our own.
- I know you are uncomfortable with some of the technology that we have recently added. The teens are really wonderful at using it. Would you be interested in a tutorial from them?
- I know how much you love to (insert any topic of interest here). Would you be willing to present a program for the teens that involves that topic?

Think of your colleagues and what makes them excited. Try to relate that to the engagement you are trying to foster in your teens. Sometimes, it just takes the right context for the value of a program to click.

Technology Resistance

The hardest part in overcoming technology resistance is often fellow staff. Change is hard and technology changes constantly. Many library staff are still struggling with the idea that they can no longer be an expert with an answer for every question. Technology has changed that aspect of librarianship forever, and recognizing that it is also changing the manner in which we program is one more way that everything is different.

Teachers and library media staff face the same issues. The school day is full of teaching to a test and behavioral issues. Little time is left to update curriculum to fit common core or the next method, let alone integrating technology. It does not help that even in school districts that are technology rich, the devices are often presented to teachers with little time for preparation of professional development to build a comfort level. Approaching technology as a facilitator rather than an expert is an excellent approach here too, but teachers can be as uncomfortable with this transition as library staff are. Connected learning in schools can help ease this discomfort by engaging the students in the process early and removing some of the anxiety and discomfort of the shift to the role of facilitator. Youth who are positively engaged with learning and each other have less time to engage in negative activities. The same outcomes are possible for schools.

Connected learning programming does not have to include technology, but it helps. It helps you connect with your teens, and it helps them connect with each other. Technology often gets a bad rap for inhibiting our connections to each other, but for youth and teens it can be a judgment-free method of collaboration. The ability to network and create has been explored in Chapter 1, and recognizing this as a key element to help teens connect can assist staff in moving beyond their comfort zone.

As previously stated, embracing the mind of a facilitator is a key element for success with connected learning. As a facilitator, you are not the expert; you are just moving the conversation or program along. You are the facilitator of any topic you want without investing the time to be an expert. Understanding the pace at which technology evolves means understanding that your expertise is now only momentary. Assuming the role of facilitator offers countless opportunities to learn about something new.

In connected learning, you are asking youth to move outside of their comfort zones and connect with other youth. So it is only fair to ask library staff to move outside of their comfort zones too. Young people are eager to demonstrate and teach what they know. What better way to engage them and build trust than to present the opportunity for them to teach you what they know about technology? Learning is a powerful motivator that can build confidence and resilience. Demonstrating the vulnerability to be willing to learn from a teen instantly makes you accessible and creates a shared bond. If staff can focus on the positive of facilitating and learning from youth or others, they can often move past their discomfort. Staff might find that they enjoy embracing their inner resilient learner too.

Making Technology Accessible

Of course, the easiest way to create staff engagement is to ensure that the most qualified and flexible staff are working on your connected learning program. Staff who understand their role as facilitators and who seek out new learning experiences every day are much more likely to embrace the goals and design of connected learning. Ultimately, library staff need to become comfortable with technology. Most of us learn every day. We learn how to cook a new recipe, use a different ATM, or care for a different plant. We learn by reading, watching YouTube, jumping in to try it, or taking a class. However, technology holds this amazing power to inspire a fear of being on the learning curve in people who would normally jump at the opportunity to learn anything else. We learn to use new things when we see their value, and connected learning has real value for libraries' ability to build more resilient youth in our communities.

If your fellow staff are still struggling with technology and the learning curve, find out what their skills and strengths are, and remind them that learning anything takes work. Nurses work to learn how to put in an IV. Knitters work to learn how to create a complicated design. None of us are experts when we first pick something up and we aren't afraid to seek out resources when it comes to learning other things. Why should technology be different? Take out a book, consult Google, or watch a YouTube video. Dig right in, or better still, ask a teen to show you.

Leveraging Partnerships and Collaborations for Support

Remember that creating a connected learning program does not have to be all on you and your library. An effective connected learning program will benefit teens across your community and likely across organizations. Plan to find partners and collaborators. Knowing where and how you like to expand your plan when and if you get support demonstrates that you have considered how the program can grow. We will explore the idea of reaching out to partners in later chapters, but it is useful to remember from the beginning of your plan that there will be opportunities to partner and collaborate to make your connected learning program stronger.

SUMMARY

You can learn a lot from a little research about your library and careful timing. Ensuring that connected learning will meet the needs of your community and organization is the first step. Looking at past and current initiatives or projects is also an excellent way to determine your administration and board of trustee's priorities and preferred method of support. Understanding current administrative and funding challenges is also beneficial to promoting your connected learning agenda at the right time.

ACTION STEPS

1. Attend a library board of trustees meeting.
2. Explore a current project or initiative. How did it gain support? Learn what made that topic important.
3. Identify a library priority to which you can tie connected learning.

3

◇ ◇ ◇

FINDING YOUR SPACE

At the North Olmsted Branch of the Cuyahoga County Public Library in suburban Cleveland, Ohio, groups of teens are clustered around tables and computers. A short walk from the community's middle school, the library sees a crowd of anywhere from 20 to 40 tweens and teens immediately after school. On any given afternoon, you can find some teens playing games, other teens chatting at tables, and still others using the library's iPads to create stop motion animation videos. To an outside bystander, this vibrant scene may appear loud and chaotic. The keen observer recognizes that learning is happening. During the hours of 2:30–6:00 p.m., the North Olmsted Library's teen space transforms into a connected learning environment.

There is not one specific, magic piece of technology or tool that transforms a space into a connected learning environment. Similarly, there is not one room design or layout that guarantees that a space will encourage connected learning. Because connected learning focuses on the interests of the learners, it can and should look dramatically different depending on the particular group of teens driving the learning experience. While the learning experiences may be different, environments that support and foster connected learning share two important characteristics: space and tools. These facets of connected learning environments are intentionally broad. By keeping these categories generic, you can define them as it best suits your library and your teens. In this chapter, we provide you with some general guidelines to help you think about how you might approach your space and tools as you build your connected learning environment.

SPACE

In an ideal world, every public library and every school library would have a dedicated teen space designed to support and encourage connected learning. This dream teen space would be flexible with mobile furniture that teens can move around and arrange to accommodate a variety of activities and group sizes. The teen space would be outfitted with state-of-the-art technology and equipment, like recording studios and fabrication equipment to empower teens to create their own projects in a safe environment. It would be staffed with a dedicated librarian to connect teens to resources to help expand their learning. Local experts and volunteers would be on hand to serve as mentors to increase the teens' knowledge and to make career connections that the teens may not have known were possible. It is OK if this description does not fit with your reality as a teen librarian. Because of available space, current policies, and/or budget, not all libraries are lucky enough to have these dream teen spaces. The good news is that regardless of your situation, you can create a space in your public library or school library that fosters connected learning. No bells and whistles are required.

In 2012, the Young Adult Library Services Association (YALSA) published the *National Teen Space Guidelines*. The YALSA guidelines include considerations for almost every aspect of teen spaces: policies, technology, collection, teen input, and furniture. While not all of the guidelines may apply to your school library or public library, this resource should be your starting point when you are ready to look at your teen space. After reading through the YALSA guidelines, talk to your teens. Teen involvement is a critical component of teen services. Whenever possible, involve the teens in your community or school in the design process. Asking teens to take part in the process ensures that the space reflects their needs and gives teens a sense of ownership for the space (Trouern-Trend et al. 2012, 3).

Including Teens in the Process

There are different ways that you can involve teens in the process of planning and implementing a library teen space that fosters connected learning. Here are a few suggestions to get you started:

- Talk with teens about the library's teen space. Ask questions about how they currently use the space and how they would like to use the space.

- Collect feedback from your teens through a survey and/or focus group. Use the data and feedback to create a plan for your teen space. Discuss the plan with your teens to ensure that it accurately reflects their needs before you move forward with purchases.

- Form a teen action group or committee that is responsible for overseeing different aspects of the teen space (e.g., furniture, display space, equipment). Give the group control of a budget and the opportunity to bring their plan to fruition.

Flexibility Is Key

Flexible spaces are nothing new in the library world. The public library meeting room is a great example. At its core, the meeting room is meant to host a variety of groups with a variety of needs. On an average day, a library meeting room might host a toddler story time in the morning, an adult book discussion in the afternoon, and a teen maker program in the evening. A public library's or school library's teen space should take a page from the meeting room and focus on flexibility.

The teen space is where teens study, hang out with friends, and participate in programs. It is important that the furniture and technology in the library's teen space accommodate these distinct types of activities (Trouern-Trend et al. 2012, 7). Having a flexible space also ensures that the space will meet the needs of your future teens. After all, the way that your teens currently use the space may be completely different from the way that future groups of teens use the space. For example, some groups of teens might view the library as a social destination. This is where they go to meet friends and hang out after school or on the weekends. Teens who view the library as a social hub might want comfortable furniture where they can sit and talk in small groups or tables where they can sit and play games. Another group of teens might view the library as the place you go to study, do homework, or work on school projects. These teens might prefer computers to work on assignments or tables where they can spread out their textbooks and study.

To ensure flexibility, stay away from heavy furniture that is permanently installed and/or difficult to move.

Here are some suggestions to consider when you are ready to outfit your space:

- *Comfortable seating.* Since a teen space needs to accommodate different types of activities, it should contain different types of furniture. Groupings of comfortable, lightweight chairs and low tables can provide teens areas to hang out, talk through and brainstorm projects, and relax.

- *Dedicated collaboration/ideation space.* Collaboration and ideation are an important part of connected learning. Try to find some space in your teen area where teens can work through ideas either in groups or on their own. Having a whiteboard or chalkboard wall and access to Post-its and markers can be a low-cost but effective way to support brainstorming and ideation.

- *Display space.* Think beyond traditional book displays. Dedicate a section of the library's teen space for teens to share their work and creations. Give control of the display space to your teens and invite them to determine what it looks like and what types of projects or artwork are displayed. If you work in a school library, make an arrangement with the art teacher to coordinate a rotating display that the students select and install in the library. In addition to featuring traditional artwork like paintings and drawings, highlight items created in STEM programs at the library. For example, host a building challenge program and display the structures that the teens create.

- *Power outlets.* It is crucial that your library's teen space has enough power outlets to accommodate both the library's technology and the teens' own devices. Make sure that power outlets can be found throughout the space. This way learning activities that need power can happen throughout the teen area, instead of being relegated to one specific area. Outlet voltage will be dependent on the equipment used. Fabrication equipment in a makerspace will have different power requirements than a laptop.

- *Shelving and storage.* Ideally, your teen collection will include resources and tools that come in a variety of formats—from traditional books and magazines to technology equipment and tools. Look for shelving and storage that not only allows you to organize and store materials but also allows teens to easily find and access resources.

- *Tables and chairs.* Look for tables and chairs that can easily be put into different configurations or be pushed aside to create open space. The furniture should be lightweight or designed to be portable (e.g., tables with wheels) so that teens and/or library staff can move things around without too much difficulty.

- *Technology.* If possible, your teen space should have access to several types of technology for the teens to find resources, create content, and share the projects that they have made.

Open Concept: More Than an HGTV Buzzword

Not all teens learn at the same pace. Connected learning works in part because teens with varying knowledge, skill levels, and experience work and learn together and alongside each other. Some teens might be brand new to a topic or field. An open space is right up there with flexibility. This allows teens to be able to hang out on the outskirts and watch an activity unfold. This lurking behavior is how teens can find out about activities in a nonthreatening and noncommittal way (Ito et al. 2013, 79). It is not uncommon to see teens engage and disengage with an activity—especially an informal activity. An accessible area and flexible furniture can accommodate this shifting number of participants in a learning activity.

No Teen Space? No Problem

You are not out of luck if your library does not have a teen space. With the right combination of flexible furniture and equipment, virtually any meeting room can easily become a connected learning space. Turn the library's meeting room into the teen zone during the after-school hours. Divide the meeting room into sections. Set up one area where teens can study or work together or independently on their own projects. Another area of the meeting room can be used for informal programs and activities facilitated by library staff, volunteers, or other teens.

Librarians in public libraries without teen spaces can also focus on outreach to meet space needs. Reach out to local schools to see if media specialists are interested in collaborating on joint connected learning programs held at school. Using the school library during a class, recess, or after school can be just as effective as holding programs in a public library. Similarly, school librarians can partner with public librarians and offer programs in public-library spaces. School librarians can also reach out to other teachers and plan activities that take place in a classroom.

TOOLS

Of all the facets of a connected learning environment, tools can be the most overwhelming. You want to make sure that you have equipment on hand that will support and increase your teens' interest and knowledge. At the same time, since tools and equipment can range in price from pretty reasonable to very expensive, make sure that whatever you purchase can be used to support a variety of learning activities. If you are not an expert in these different subject areas, it can be hard to determine exactly what you need. Compounding your stress can be the fact that there is always going to be a newer, better, more expensive piece of technology that would be a great addition to your space. How do you ensure that you purchase the right tools and equipment that have broad appeal and support a variety interests? (This is assuming that you have a budget to purchase equipment and tools, which is not always the case.)

Start with the Basics

Laptop or desktop computers should be the first thing on your list. Tablets, such as iPads, should be a close second. Although they are not super exciting as far as equipment goes, tablets and computers are more versatile and useful than any other piece of equipment you are likely to get for your teen space. They also support the flexibility that is central to connected learning. Apps and other software can support teens' learning and interests both during and outside of library programs. And while software like Adobe Photoshop and Adobe Illustrator are fantastic, there is plenty of quality free software available on a variety of topics, from coding to music editing to 3D design.

After purchasing basic equipment like computers and tablets, look at your budget to determine the remaining equipment and tools you will purchase. Find out what your teens are interested in and find equipment to support their interests. Whether you are interested in creating a makerspace or are just looking for some additional equipment to support programs and activities, there are many great resources and lists available online.

Recommended Equipment and Technology

When it comes to choosing equipment and technology to support connected learning, you could go in many different directions. Below is a list of recommendations that can be used to support a variety of subjects and interests. Consider your budget and the interests of your teens. Recommendations have been divided into the following categories: tools, electronics equipment, robotics equipment, production equipment, and fabrication equipment. Please note that the prices listed for these products may change.

TOOLS

Hand tools are incredibly versatile. A variety of tools can enable you to offer engaging programs like take-apart tech or chain reaction challenges. Tools also give teens an opportunity to tinker with and create their own items.

- Clamps
- Drill
- Glue gun
- Hammers
- Handsaw

- Level
- Pliers
- Rulers
- Rotary cutter
- Scissors
- Screwdrivers (be sure to get a variety of sizes of slotted, phillips, and torx screwdrivers)
- T-square
- Tape measure
- Utility knife
- Wire cutter, crimper, stripper
- Wrench

ELECTRONICS EQUIPMENT

- Arduino ($24.95 for Arduino Uno R3). Arduino is an open-source electronics platform. Users create projects with an Arduino board and the Arduino software.
- Bare Conductive Electric Paint ($29.95 for a 50-mL jar). Paint your own circuits—a great way to incorporate art into your electronics projects.
- Chibitronics Chibi Lights LED Circuit Stickers STEM Starter Kit ($30). Introduce teens to circuits with Chibitronics Chibi Lights Circuit Stickers. The kit comes with a sketchbook that walks users through different types of circuits (e.g., simple circuit, parallel circuit, and switches). Each kit includes copper tape, LED light stickers, and a coin battery.
- Circuit Scribe Conductive Ink Pen ($9.99). A conductive ink pen that allows you to easily draw your own circuits.
- littleBits ($39.95 to $4,999, depending on the kit). littleBits are electronic building blocks that can be used to create a variety of inventions. The website has great resources for educators, including lessons and samples projects.
- Makey Makey Classic ($49.95). An invention kit that replaces a computer keyboard with any conductive material (from bananas to play doh to copper tape to humans). The Makey Makey connects to a computer via the USB port. Since a Makey Makey replaces a computer keyboard, it can be used with a variety of programs and software, including MIT's Scratch. There is no specific Makey Makey software required.
- Raspberry Pi 3 Model B ($35.00). A single-board computer developed by the Raspberry Pi Foundation to teach computer science and programming. Raspberry Pis can be used for a variety of projects, from a retro gaming console to a photo booth.
- Snap Circuits ($34.95 to $149.95, depending on the kit). Users learn about circuits and elementary engineering concepts with a kit that includes components that can be snapped together in different combinations to create different projects.
- Squishy Circuits ($30.00 for the standard kit). The kit teaches basic electronics concepts with conductive and insulating dough. The kit includes LEDs, buzzer,

motor, switch, and a recipe for both types of dough. The dough can be made from common kitchen ingredients.

ROBOTICS EQUIPMENT

- Dash & Dot Wonder Pack ($279.99). These are interactive robots that teach coding skills. Program the robots using apps on your phone or a tablet. The apps are compatible with iOS devices, Android devices, and Kindle devices. The Wonder Pack includes both the Dash and Dot robots plus additional accessories.
- LEGO Education WeDo 2.0 ($189.95 per core set). Participants build simple machines using LEGO pieces, motors, and sensors and create a program to run their machines using LEGO Education drag-and-drop software. You will likely need one core set for each pair of teens.
- LEGO MINDSTORMS EV3 ($411.95 per core set): This is a programmable robotics kit. Participants build a robot using LEGO pieces, sensors, and motors. Participants create programs for the robots using LEGO EV3 drag-and-drop software. You will likely need one core set for each pair of teens.

PRODUCTION EQUIPMENT

- Chromakey green screen backdrop and stand (prices will vary). With a portable green screen, teens can add a creative twist to their photos and movies. Affordable green screen apps like Green Screen by Do Ink make it easy to use green screens in projects.
- Blue Yeti USB microphone ($129.99). This is a portable microphone with good audio quality that can be used for a portable recording studio.
- Video camera (prices will vary). If you have teens interested in video production, you should invest in a video camera. While you could use a smart phone or tablet camera, you will get better quality video with a dedicated video camera. Be sure to also purchase a tripod and a lighting kit for the camera.

FABRICATION EQUIPMENT

- Cricut (prices range from $149.99 to $399.99 depending on the model). The Cricut is a cutting machine that can cut a variety of materials, including vinyl, paper, textiles, leather, and foam.
- Heat press (prices will vary). This is used in conjunction with other fabrication equipment like a Cricut or vinyl cutter to make T-shirts, bags, and other accessories.
- Sewing machine (prices will vary). Sewing machines can support a variety of projects from fashion to design to wearable circuits.
- Structure Sensor 3D Scanner ($379–$399 depending on iPad model; price does not include the iPad). This is a handheld 3D scanner that attaches to an iPad. Use the scanner to support 3D design programs, virtual reality programs, and/or augmented reality programs.
- 3D printer (prices will vary; most will range from $1,000 to $2,500). There are a variety of 3D printers on the market. MakerBot, Ultimaker, and LulzBot are some of the more popular manufacturers. When deciding which model to go

with, consider what type of material you would like to print with (e.g., PLA filament or ABS filament) and what type of software is required for the printer.

- Carvey by Inventables ($2,499.00): Carvey is a desktop CNC routing machine created for classroom use.

- Laser cutter (prices will vary but expect to spend $1,000+ depending on the manufacturer). This is an expensive piece of equipment. If you purchase from a top-rated vendor like Epilog Laser, expect to pay about $8,000 for the entry-level model. While a laser cutter could easily be the most expensive piece of equipment you purchase for your library, it is also extremely versatile. A laser cutter can cut or engrave a variety of materials with precision. It is a great piece of equipment for prototyping.

Whatever equipment you end up purchasing for your library, make sure that you also have the appropriate safety equipment and safety guidelines in place for your space. General safety equipment may include safety glasses, dust masks, earplugs, aprons, and gloves. Your space should also have a first aid kit and a fire extinguisher.

Don't Underestimate the Importance of Your Collection

Your teen collection, both physical and online, is one of the most important tools at your disposal. Just like your teen space, your collection should
be flexible and reflect your teens' interests and needs. Make sure that your
teen collection includes a variety of formats (e.g., books, magazines, audio
and video content, databases) (Braun et al. 2014, 15). Think beyond traditional physical and online materials. Chapter 4 includes more details
about how you can evaluate and expand your collection to support connected learning.

How Do You Pay for All of This Stuff?

Limited budgets are a reality at most libraries. Here are four suggestions when
you are looking for funding:

PARTNER WITH COLLEAGUES

When examining your budget, think strategically and see if you can combine
some of your funds with another department to purchase items and equipment. If you work in the teen department at a public library, is it possible to combine some of your funds with the children's department to purchase equipment
that can be used to support the programs and collections for both age groups?
If you are a school librarian, reach out to some classroom teachers to see if you
can create a partnership. Perhaps you can combine some of the library's funds
with a classroom teacher's funds to buy equipment that could be used in lessons

in the classroom and by tweens and teens in the school's media center outside of class time.

LOCAL BUSINESSES

Reach out to local businesses. Some businesses may offer grants or sponsorships for programs. You may also be able to arrange an in-kind donation, which means that the business would provide goods or services instead of a monetary donation.

YALSA's partnering toolkit *Partnering to Increase Your Impact* contains valuable information on finding and approaching local organizations and businesses to forge a partnership: http://www.ala.org/yalsa/sites/ala.org.yalsa/files/content/Partnerships_WebVersion.pdf

CROWDFUNDING

Crowdfunding allows a person or organization to leverage social networks to raise funds for a product or project during a specified amount of time. The fundraising campaign is held using online platforms where multiple donors can contribute funds toward the project. Campaigns could range from money for a medical procedure to a honeymoon to equipment for a library program.

There are a lot of crowdfunding platforms out there. Check out the different platforms to see which one is the best fit for your organization or campaign. Some platforms cater to specific industries while others may be an "all-or-nothing" platform, which means if your campaign does not reach its goal, you do not receive any of the pledged funds.

Here are some of the most popular crowdfunding platforms:

- Kickstarter: www.kickstarter.com
- Indiegogo: www.indiegogo.com
- GoFundMe: www.gofundme.com
- Donors Choose: www.donorschoose.org

GRANTS

Grants can be a great way to fund a project or program. Here are some resources that you can use when searching for potential grants and/or funders:

- Institute of Museum and Library Services: https://www.imls.gov/grants
- Visualizing Funding for Libraries Data Tool: http://libraries.foundationcenter.org/
- YALSA Funding, Awards and Grants wiki article: http://wikis.ala.org/yalsa/index.php/Funding,_Awards_and_Grants

VIRTUAL ENVIRONMENTS

When you are thinking about the teen space at your school library or your public library, make sure that you are not only thinking about the physical space. To fully examine connected learning environments, it is important to look beyond physical environments to virtual environments too. Today's teens live in a connected world. To say that teens spend a great deal of their time online is an understatement. The Pew Research Center's report *Teens, Social Media & Technology Overview 2015* found that 92 percent of teens go online daily and 24 percent of teens go online "almost constantly" (Lenhart 2015, 2). While connected learning does not require technology, the connections and resources that teens can make using digital tools can greatly expand their learning experiences (Ito et al. 2013, 82). If a teen's peer group at school or at the library does not share a teen's interest, he or she can find resources and community spaces online that meet those needs.

Just as you would strive to include teens in the creation of the physical space, teens should also be involved in the design and creation of the library's virtual space. The space should be interactive and allow teens to "share their work, receive feedback and build community" (Trouern-Trend et al. 2012, 8). Creating and supporting a teen-centered and teen-created online space may not be realistic for every public library and school library. It can also seem like a complicated or daunting task. Start small and be realistic. Does your library have a blog where you share news and other information with your teens? Consider empowering teens to create content and manage the blog. The same goes for the library's social media platforms. If possible, see if teens could be involved with running those spaces.

If you cannot create a virtual space for your library, look for other online resources and communities for teens. Staying current can be an ongoing challenge, but remember that you can look to your teens for this information too. Find out what online communities and resources your teens use and share this information with other teens who might be interested.

SUMMARY

Teens need their own space. The space should be a safe place, where teens can come together to learn, connect, and share. Ideally, this space is permanent and intended for teen use only. If you cannot create a dedicated physical teen space in your library, see if you can adapt other library spaces (e.g., a meeting room) into part-time teen spaces during library programs or during certain hours each day.

ACTION STEPS

1. Begin to involve teens in your teen space design or planning. If your library has a teen space, involve teens in discussions about

maintenance or updates. If your library does not have a teen space, talk with teens about ways to foster a sense of space in your existing library.

2. Evaluate the tools you currently own or can access. Determine if there are any holes in the collection, and brainstorm for ways that you can meet this need (e.g., use existing budget to purchase tools, find community partners that can provide access to the tools, or search for alternative funding like grants or a crowd-sourcing campaign to raise funds for the tools).

3. Evaluate your library's virtual space. If you do not have a virtual space, find online communities and resources that you can share with teens.

4

◆ ◆ ◆

DEVELOPING YOUR COLLECTION

Connected learning encourages teens to actively explore their interests. Library programs are a fantastic way to introduce teens to new topics and to continue to support their learning, and a library's collection sustains learning all the time. The resources in your library's collection are always available for your teens to access; they are not dependent on staff or volunteers to facilitate a learning activity. This chapter will explore how you can expand your collection development policy beyond traditional library materials, to include apps, online resources and tools, and equipment and technology.

EXPANDING YOUR COLLECTION DEVELOPMENT POLICY TO INCLUDE DIGITAL MEDIA

When was the last time you reviewed your library's collection development policy? Does your library's collection development policy include items outside traditional library materials like books and movies? It might be time to consider expanding your collection development policy to include digital media tools like apps or other special collections like technology or tools. Apps and software can be a great place to start to expand your collection development policy.

If you are still on the fence about creating a digital media collection for your library, consider recent compelling research about mobile device usage. As of 2016, more people were using mobile devices like smart phones and tablets to access the Internet than computers (StatCounter Global Stats 2016). This trend is not limited to adults. In 2015, the PEW Research Center reported that 73 percent of teens have access to a smart phone and 58 percent of teens have access to a tablet (Lenhart et al. 2015, 8–11). Mobile apps can be an asset to any library's connected learning program. Not only can apps extend learning activities in your programs and in your teen space, but apps are also relatively inexpensive.

As your public library or school library begins to purchase apps for tablets, you should consider how you can incorporate apps into your library's collection development policy. While there is literature and guidance about including electronic resources like databases in a collection development policy, there is still very little available about including apps in a library's collection development policy (Arzola and Havelka 2015, 44). Below are some areas commonly included in well-rounded collection development policies. Each category includes questions and considerations for you to think about as you develop a collection development policy for your app collection.

Consider Your Library's Mission Statement

Before you amend your collection development policy to include digital media like apps and online tools, you need to be clear on how using these resources will support the mission of your library. It is important to make sure that your programs and purchases align with your library's mission. If teen programs and services are considered a core function of your library, then you could argue that providing access to high-quality apps to further teen learning aligns with your mission. Here are some important questions to consider as you design your app collection:

- What is the purpose of your library's app collection?
- Are you purchasing apps for a specific platform (iOS, Android)? If so, what platform will the library use?
- What age level will use the app collection?
- How will customers access the apps?
- Are the apps used by staff in library programs, or do you have devices that teens can check out and use on their own?

Selection Criteria

App Review Resources

Just like you rely on reviews when selecting traditional materials like books and movies for your library collection, it is important to have reputable resources for finding apps. Look beyond the app store for reviews. Here is a list of several resources for app reviews:

- AASL: Best Apps for Teaching & Learning
- *Children's Technology Review*
- Common Sense Media App Reviews
- *The Horn Book*: App Review of the Week
- *School Library Journal* App Reviews

Evaluation Criteria

When deciding to purchase apps for your collection, you will need to evaluate the apps. For the most part, you will use the same evaluation criteria for apps that you would use when evaluating books for your library collection. Sure, there are criteria that are format specific, like usability, but other factors (e.g., authority, content, currency) are the same regardless of format. Here are some factors to consider during your evaluation:

- Accessibility: Is the app available in multiple languages?
- Authority: Who are the app creators and/or developers? Is it easy to identify and find contact information for the creators?
- Content: Is the app content age appropriate? Does the app include advertisements? Are there support materials for users and/or parents and educators?
- Cost: What is the cost of the app? Does the app include in-app purchases?
- Currency: Is the app up to date and relevant? When was the app developed? When did the developer last release an update?
- Privacy: Does the app protect user information? Can users easily leave the app and access social media or the Internet?
- Usability: Is the app easy to navigate and free of glitches?

Collection Maintenance

After selecting apps for your library's app collection, determine how often you will review your collection. Because mobile technology is constantly changing, you may want to review and weed your app collection more regularly than you maintain other areas of your collection. You also may need to think out of the box when it comes to measuring usage for your app collection. Because of the nature of an app collection, it may be hard to collect usage statistics for specific apps. One possible solution is to develop a survey for your app collection to find out from customers and staff what apps they are using and what they think of the apps. While you will not get responses from everyone using the collection, a survey can still provide you with some useful data.

Budget

While apps can be affordable, you want to have flexibility to update the collection as you discover new apps. Do you have a budget that can support your app collection? How is the budget determined? Is it based on the number of devices that you own, or is it based on the age level of customers (e.g., there is an overall budget for teen materials that includes a line item for apps)?

When you determine your app budget, be sure to build in funds for review apps. Use reputable review sources like those listed above to create a list of apps that you want to look at more closely. Then purchase one copy of each of the apps on your list to review. It is important to have some hands-on time with the apps to make sure that they suit your needs—especially before you buy copies of paid apps for many devices.

If you do not have a budget, you can still create and maintain an app collection for your library. There are certainly a number of free apps available on all mobile platforms. If you do not have a budget, you can conceivably create a collection with free apps. Be aware that using free apps may come with some limitations. Free apps often have ads. As you are evaluating the apps, make sure that you look at the ads. Are the ads appropriate? Free apps also might be an abbreviated version of the app, where the paid version has more content available. Neither ads nor limited content is necessarily a deal breaker. You can absolutely find quality free apps; you just may need to be aware of additional considerations.

You also may be able to get paid apps for a discounted rate. App developers sometimes offer discounts for educators. Apps occasionally go on sale too. It is not uncommon for developers to make a usually paid app free for one or two days as a sales tactic. Get on the mailing list for your favorite app developers so that you can receive notifications about special offers and sales.

RECOMMENDED APPS

Once you have decided to include apps in your collection, it is helpful to have a list to get you started. Look at the apps below and use the suggested evaluation criteria to determine if these apps should be added to your collection.

Animation Apps

- Autodesk SketchBook by Autodesk, Inc. (free: iOS and Android): Autodesk SketchBook is a digital drawing app. It includes a variety of different drawing implements to choose from, and it has a clean and easy-to-use interface. It is a great resource for teens interested in art and animation.

- Toontastic 3D by Google, Inc. (free: iOS and Android). Toontastic 3D is a storytelling app where users can create their own cartoons, animations, and stories. The app has preloaded characters and scenes, but users can also use the camera and/or a drawing tool to create their own characters. Users are guided through the storytelling process with a story arc tool that breaks down the distinct parts of the story.

Coding Apps

- Hopscotch by Hopscotch Technologies (free with optional monthly subscription: iOS only): The Hopscotch app has a variety of lessons using drag-and-drop coding to teach basic logic skills. Users can create and share projects with the Hopscotch community.

- Swift Playgrounds by Apple (free: iOS): Lessons and challenges teach users how to code with Swift, an open language that can be used to build apps for iOS, Mac, Apple TV, and Apple Watch. Swift can also be used to create code for a variety of robots and drones including LEGO MINDSTORMS EV3, Sphero, and Dash.

- Tynker: Coding for Kids. Programming Made Easy! by Tynker (free with in-app purchases: iOS and Android): Tynker uses visual code blocks reminiscent of MIT Media Lab's Scratch to teach logic and coding skills. The app includes seasonal projects, Hour of Code lessons, and lessons in a variety of subject areas, including animation, games, storytelling, and physics. The free version grants access to a couple of tutorials in each category, but the rest of the tutorials are available for purchase. Tynker can also be used to create programs for drones and robots, including LEGO Education WeDo 2.0, Sphero, and Parrot Minidrones.

Filmmaking Apps

- Green Screen by Do Ink by DK Pictures, Inc. ($2.99: iOS): Green Screen by Do Ink offers a straightforward way to create movies and pictures with green screen technology. While the app is intuitive, a sample project tutorial walks users through the basic steps. Projects can be saved to the device camera roll.

- iMovie by Apple (free: iOS only): Apple's iMovie app offers a relatively easy way to make professional-looking movies and movie trailers. Users can import their own content or use the device camera to take pictures and videos or record audio while in the app.

- Stop Motion Studio Pro by Cateater, LLC ($4.99: iOS): Features like green screen technology, a photo editor, a sound editor, and the ability to add a theme with titles and credits allow users to easily make great stop motion movies.

Music Editing Apps

- GarageBand by Apple (free, iOS only): Probably the most popular music app for iPad, GarageBand makes it easy for users to create music. With Smart Instruments and the updated Live Loops feature, even users who are not professional musicians can create their own professional-sounding songs.

RECOMMENDED FREE ONLINE TOOLS AND RESOURCES

If you are ready to expand your collection to digital media and resources, you are not limited to apps. There are a lot of free online tools and resources that you install on your computers. These resources are great for programs and for teens to explore and learn on their own. Make sure that you periodically check for new updates—particularly if you create guides or tutorials for using the software. Updates may change the appearance or functionality. You should be mindful of any changes—especially if you plan to use the software in library programs.

Animation

- Krita: https://krita.org/en/. Krita is a robust, open-source digital art and animation tool.

Coding

- Arduino Create: https://create.arduino.cc/. Arduino Create is an online platform that enables you to manage your Arduino projects. You can access resources, tools, and tutorials to help you navigate through the stages of your project development.

- Code.org: https://code.org/. This is a great resource when you are starting with coding. The website includes sample lessons, research on the importance of teaching computer science, and resources.

- Codecademy: https://www.codecademy.com/. This includes lessons on a variety of programming languages, including HTML, JavaScript, Python, and Ruby. This is a great resource for teens who are ready to move beyond Scratch and other visual block-based coding programs.

- Scratch: https://scratch.mit.edu. Created by the Lifelong Kindergarten Group at MIT Media Lab, Scratch is a visual programming tool where users can create games, art, and music creations. Scratch has a built-in community where users can choose to publicly share their projects. Users can also find and remix other programs to make them their own. Scratch can be used with other technology, including Makey Makeys and LEGO Education WeDos.

- W3Schools: https://www.w3schools.com. W3schools is a free web development site with tutorials on languages like HTML, CSS, and JavaScript.

3D Design

- Blender: https://www.blender.org/. Blender is an open-source 3D software. Blender can be used for 3D modeling, 3D animation, rendering, and game creation.

- Circuits on Tinkercad: https://www.tinkercad.com/circuits. Integrate real electronic components into 3D designs created in Tinkercad.

- SketchUp Make: https://www.sketchup.com/. A 3D design tool designed for K–12 students, SketchUp Make is easy to use and could be used as an alternative to or alongside of software like Tinkercad in a 3D design program.

- Tinkercad: https://www.tinkercad.com. This is a simple, online CAD (computer-aided design) tool created by Autodesk. Users create 3D designs by grouping simple shapes together. Tinkercad also has a built-in online community where users can find and remix designs or share their own designs.

- Thingiverse: https://www.thingiverse.com/. This website is MakerBot's 3D community where users can find and share design files for 3D printing or laser cutting.

Music Editing and Creation

- Audacity: http://www.audacityteam.org/. Audacity is a comprehensive, online music editor that lets you import audio, record audio, and add effects, to name just a few features.
- Chrome Music Lab: https://musiclab.chromeexperiments.com/. Chrome Music Lab uses hands-on experiments to teach musical concepts in an intuitive and fun way.

Photo Editor/Image Editor

- GIMP: https://www.gimp.org/. GIMP is an image manipulation program that can be used for animation, photo editing, or graphic design.
- Pixlr Editor: https://pixlr.com/editor/. Pixlr is a browser-based photo editor. It is a great free alternative to Adobe Photoshop.

Vector Graphics Editor

- Inkscape: https://inkscape.org/en/. Inkscape is a free open-source vector graphics editor. This is a great alternative to Adobe Illustrator.

OTHER EQUIPMENT AND TECHNOLOGY

While this chapter focused mostly on digital resources and tools, these are not the only items that can be added to a library's collection. When you are evaluating your collection, really look at when and how teens can access resources like tablets, robots, or Raspberry Pis. Are these items only available during programs? Can teens in your community access the items at school or at home? If teens in your community cannot easily access these resources, tablets, or tools, consider expanding your collection to include these types of items. If you decide to include equipment or tools in your collection development policy, you can apply the same basic principles used when including digital media. Refer to the Recommended

Equipment and Technology section in Chapter 3 for specific suggestions and ideas of the type of equipment to add to your program.

Unusual Circulating Collections

From technology and kits to musical instruments to tools, several libraries have created unique circulating collections. Here are a few examples:

- Ann Arbor District Library, Michigan: http://www.aadl.org/catalog/browse/unusual. The Ann Arbor Public Library has an extensive collection of unusual circulating items. Categories include the following:
  - Art tools: Sewing machines, digital drawing tablets, spinning wheel
  - Music tools: Electric guitars, pedals, theremin
  - Science tools: Microscopes, telescopes, Makey Makey, Arduino starter kit
- Cuyahoga County Public Library, Ohio: http://www.cuyahogalibrary.org/Borrow/Toys-and-Story-Kits.aspx. The Cuyahoga County Public Library circulates toys and games for children from birth up to age 10.
- Fayetteville Free Public Library, New York: https://www.fflib.org/kits-technology. The Fayetteville Free Public Library offers a variety of equipment that can be checked out and used while customers are in the library. Equipment includes digital cameras and videos, Dash robots, and STEM kits like Snap Circuits and littleBits.
- Lopez Island Library, Washington: http://lopezlibrary.org/music. The Lopez Island Public Library has a collection of musical instruments that can be checked out for a month. The library's collection includes violins, guitars, keyboards, French horns, and ukuleles.
- Oakland Public Library, California: http://www.oaklandlibrary.org/locations/tool-lending-library. The Oakland Public Library has a collection of over 5,000 tools that customers can check out.

Connected Learning in Action: Expanding Access through a Joint Public Library/School Library Collection in North Royalton, Ohio

Laura Whitehead, the media specialist at the North Royalton Middle School and North Royalton High School in suburban Cleveland, Ohio, and Shannon Sanek, the teen librarian at the North Royalton Branch of the Cuyahoga County Public Library (CCPL), regularly work together to serve the teens in their community. In addition to sharing ideas and resources, Shannon and Laura create and co-facilitate monthly programs at the middle school. In 2016, Shannon and Laura found an opportunity to expand their partnership when CCPL offered grants to staff looking to create innovative programs and services. Together, Laura and Shannon submitted a grant proposal for a joint collection that would be housed at the North Royalton schools. The collection would include equipment and technology like Raspberry Pis, 3D pens, and mini drones that teachers in the schools could use in their classes. While CCPL owns the equipment, it lives in a deposit collection in the schools.

SUMMARY

The library is the great equalizer. Everyone has access to the same resources, regardless of socioeconomic status. This is most evident in a library's collection. Embrace the power of your library's collection and consider expanding your collection development policy to include materials and resources beyond books, databases, and movies. If it aligns with your library's mission, begin to include equipment, apps, and other online resources that can further teens' interests. Having additional tools and resources for teens to access will only continue to support their learning.

ACTION STEPS

1. Evaluate your current collection. What subject areas need additional information? Create a plan that includes a budget and timeline for how you will build these areas of your collection.

2. Reach out to your customers to find out what types of items they would like to see added to your library's collection. Collect customer feedback both informally through conversations and formally through surveys and suggestion forms.

3. Review your library's collection development policy. If you decide to add unusual items to your collection, update your policy to include these items.

5

◇ ◇ ◇

STAFFING AND RUNNING
THE PROGRAM

A huge component of connected learning is the connections that teens make with other people and the information that they learn from these individuals. While Chapter 6 will delve into creating and facilitating programs that reflect teens' interests, this chapter focuses on the people who facilitate the programs. In most libraries, staff create and run library programs. Staff might be hesitant to offer programs on topics that they are uncomfortable or unfamiliar with, even if teens are interested in the topic. This chapter will include information about how staff mind-set may need to shift to fully embrace connected learning.

Library staff are not the only people who can effectively facilitate teen connected learning programs. If possible, public libraries and school libraries should work with volunteers who can make real-world, career connections to teens' interests. Since working with volunteers may be new for some libraries, this chapter also includes information on why you should use volunteers and how you can create a volunteer program at your library.

SHIFTING STAFF MIND-SET

Staff as Educators

If you were asked to come up with a list of professions who could be considered educators, who would come to mind? Would you think of classroom teachers? Or perhaps you think of experts in certain fields or subject areas? While educators can certainly be subject experts, having a teaching certificate is not a requirement for subject expertise. Educators are people who guide and facilitate a person's learning. Sure, classroom teachers, college professors, and other "traditional" educators fit this definition. But by removing the expectation of expertise and replacing it with that of guidance and facilitation, your view of educators can expand to include other professions.

What about library staff? Libraries are universally recognized as institutions of lifelong learning. Customers come to libraries for information, and it is library staff who provide access to that information. This information can take the form of library materials like books and DVDs, or it can be online resources, or it can even be library programs. By connecting customers to this information, library staff members are facilitating learning for their customers (Kepple 2013, 33). So, yes, library staff are absolutely educators. This is a role that library staff should embrace proudly!

Staff as Lifelong Learners

If libraries are institutions of lifelong learning, then library staff need to consider themselves lifelong learners as well. Library staff with curiosity and passion about learning will bring that excitement and enthusiasm to the learning activities that they facilitate for teens. Not to mention that approaching learning experiences from the perspective of a lifelong learner may make you a more comfortable and confident facilitator. To foster lifelong learning in staff, public libraries and school libraries need to make a commitment to professional development and learning opportunities. This cannot be something that an organization gives lip service to. Librarians need to truly create a culture of learning. In her article "Creating a Culture of Learning at Your Library," Kate McNair asks libraries to "create a culture that doesn't punish failure, that encourages reflection and improvement, and asks staff to share what they have learned. The sooner we recognize that we all fail, the better we can serve teens (who have a long life of failure ahead of them)" (McNair 2016, 30).

Staff as Facilitators

No one has all the answers. As just mentioned, you can view yourself as an educator without having all the answers. Lack of expertise should not prevent you from offering library programs on subjects that you are not familiar with. Sure, it may be uncomfortable—and even scary—to offer a program on a subject you do not know. Yet, when you embrace connected learning programs in your library, this is exactly what you need to do. How? Start thinking of yourself as a facilitator, not as an expert. According to Sam Kaner's book *Facilitator's Guide to Participatory Decision-Making*, "the facilitator's job is to support everyone to do their best thinking" (Kaner 2014, 32). So how can you employ facilitation techniques in your teen programs? Here are some guidelines:

- *Start with an icebreaker.* Do not assume that all the teens in your program know each other. Public librarians in particular may have teens from different schools, different communities, and different grade levels in a teen program. Sure, icebreakers can be cheesy, but they are also a way to even the playing field in a program. The activity might be lame but everyone (including you!) is completing the silly activity together.

- *Set clear ground rules and expectations.* First spell out the plan for the learning activity. This can be as simple as communicating the program goal (e.g., "Today we are going to create a paper circuit"). After communicating the goal, as a group, determine the rules and expectations for the learning experience. Asking the teens to create the rules and expectations for the program allows the teens to direct their own learning.

- *Be prepared, but be flexible.* Removing the expectation of expertise does not give you license to go into a library program unprepared. As you plan your learning experience, take the time to do background research, conduct a run through of the program, and make any needed adjustments. Be as prepared as possible, but recognize that you will never be able to plan for every eventuality. Be ready to switch up the activity if something does not work as planned, or if the group does not respond to a portion of the activity.

- *Read the room.* Be mindful of the teens attending your program. If you notice that some teens are not engaged in the activity, try to redirect their attention. If the entire group does not seem engaged in the activity, be ready to switch things up. This might mean that you throw your original plan out the window. That is OK. This happens to everyone at some point. If you find yourself in this situation, ask the teens for ideas on how the group can adjust the learning activity.

- *Be confident, but be vulnerable.* Manage and guide the activity, but do not be afraid to admit when you do not have information. Remember, you are not the expert in the room; you are learning with the group. This is another fantastic opportunity to engage your teens and invite them to share their knowledge.

- *Ask questions instead of providing answers.* When teens have questions or encounter challenges, resist the temptation to give them the answer. Instead, ask open-ended questions to guide their learning. If or when teens get stuck during an activity, ask questions like "What have you tried so far?" to get teens to think about their process. Encourage the teens to work together to solve challenges. Questions like "Has anyone else encountered this program?" What did you do to resolve it?" and "Any ideas about what he/ she could try next?" can jumpstart conversations between teens.

Connected learning should give teens an opportunity to share their knowledge with their peers and with you. Your lack of expertise is not a shortcoming. It is a chance for you to empower your teens! If your teens are interested in design, chances are they have already picked up some skills. Give those teens a chance to run with the program.

SEEKING OUTSIDE EXPERTS

Supporting teens' interests and introducing teens to new topics through resources and programs is a great start to fostering connected learning in your library. While you might have wrapped your head around the concepts of connected learning, it can be a challenge to put the framework into practice. Shifting your mind-set around programming may take some time. That is OK! It can be uncomfortable to change your thinking from library staff as the expert in the room to library staff as program facilitator—especially when you offer programs on subjects that you do not have experience in. However, you and your staff do not need to go about this alone. Seeking outside experts to lend their expertise or even lead programs can be a huge asset to your library's connected learning program.

Remember that relationships are at the heart of the future of both library services and connected learning. As stated in YALSA's report *The Future of Library Services for and with Teens: A Call to Action*:

Library service for and with teens in the future are not librarian-based or book-based or even place-based. They are centered on relationships—relationships between teens and library staff, between library staff and the broader community. These relationships result in connections; connections that allow libraries to create an ever-changing collection of programs and services that meet the requirements of individual teens and teen groups at any moment of need. (Braun et al. 2014, 11)

Volunteers can be a great asset to your library's connected learning program, and, on a broader scale, volunteers can be a great asset to your organization. Here are some reasons why you should consider using volunteers in your teen library programs:

- Volunteers can serve as mentors for your teens.
- Volunteers can become advocates.
- Investing in a volunteer program is an investment in your community.

Volunteers as Mentors

When young adults have supportive adults in their life, they are more likely to remain in school, even when facing adverse life experiences (Center for Promise 2015, 15). These types of supportive relationships are a critical component of healthy adolescent development. The Search Institute identified 40 factors that contribute to healthy adolescent development. Known as the *40 Developmental Assets for Adolescents*, library programs that include library staff and other community volunteers can satisfy several of the assets. The most obvious are as follows (Search Institute 2007):

- Other adult relationships: Young person receives support from three or more nonparent adults.
- Community values youth: Young person perceives that adults in the community value youth.
- Adult role models: Parent(s) and other adults model positive, responsible behavior.
- Youth programs: Young person spends three or more hours per week in sports, clubs, or organizations at school and/or in community organizations.

By using volunteers as mentors in teen-connected learning programs, you are not only supporting your teens' interests but also supporting your teens' healthy development.

Mentoring has a positive impact on a teen's life. In 2014, MENTOR: The National Mentoring Partnership released the report *The Mentoring Effect: Young People's Perspective on the Outcomes and Availability of Mentoring*. This report marked the first time a survey sought to get young people's opinion on their experiences with mentoring (Bruce and Bridgeland 2014, 1). The report confirmed the value of mentoring—particularly with at-risk youth. Young adults who had mentors were more likely to attend college and set higher educational goals than young people who did not have mentors. In fact, 76 percent of at-risk young adults who had a mentor planned to graduate from college versus 56 percent of at-risk young adults who did not have a mentor. Young adults with mentors also valued the mentoring relationships and saw them as providing support and guidance (Bruce and Bridgeland 2014, 3). While the positive outcomes are great, the report also revealed a mentoring gap. One in three young adults reported that they never had a mentor. "Nationwide, that means today approximately 16 million youth, including nine million at-risk youth, will reach age 19 without ever having a mentor" (Bruce and Bridgeland 2014, 5). Library connected learning programs can help address this mentoring gap by putting these youth in contact with supportive adults in library programs.

Volunteers as Advocates

Dedicated volunteers can become some of your library's best advocates. If a volunteer has a positive experience helping out during programs at his or her local public library or school library, he or she is likely to talk about these experiences with the other people in his or her life. This is wonderful publicity that can have some great benefits. Some of these benefits include:

- *Teens need advocates.* Teens are very often a marginalized group or feel that they are. They need to have adults who support and advocate for them.
- *Volunteers can help you attract new audiences.* A volunteer's network likely includes non-library users. When volunteers talk about their positive experiences, they are potentially promoting your programs and services to people whom you do not currently reach.
- *Volunteers can become donors.* Volunteers are already investing their time at your library and in your program. If they have a positive experience, they may consider making a financial contribution to your library.

Volunteers as a Community Investment

Libraries should reflect and support their communities. By creating a program where supportive adults can share their knowledge and expertise with teens, libraries are showing their commitment to the youth in their community. Libraries are also demonstrating that they value the talents and expertise of their community's local experts.

Where Do You Find Volunteers?

Before you begin recruiting volunteers, you need to determine the goal of your volunteer program. Are you hoping to find volunteers who have knowledge in specific subject areas like engineering or software development? Or maybe you are trying to find volunteers who have certain skills like photo editing or painting? Or perhaps you are looking for adults in the community who can positively engage with your teens in the library after school. Do you want volunteers to help you in specific programs, or are you hoping that the volunteers will plan and facilitate their own programs? These are the types of questions that you need to ask yourself as you are thinking through this process. Take the time to really consider what you are looking for in potential volunteers. The clearer and more specific your defined needs, the more likely you will find appropriate volunteers. That being said, make sure your focus is not too narrow. This could also make it difficult to find volunteers. For instance, let's say you are hoping to find volunteers to help during a LEGO robotics program. If you limit your search to volunteers who have experience using the LEGO software, you may not have any luck finding a volunteer. Instead, expand your search to include volunteers with programming, engineering, or robotics experience. You will likely have much better luck finding appropriate volunteers, and your teens will still have an opportunity to learn specialized knowledge from experts. If anything, it will actually make for a stronger library program if your teens see that knowledge can be translated to different platforms or tools. This is an important life skill to learn.

Once you have determined the types of volunteers you are looking for, you can start your search. Here's how:

- *Reach out to your existing network.* Start with the people you know. Talk to colleagues who work in different departments and ask them if they have knowledge or expertise that they would be willing to share with teens. If you work in a public library, attend a board of trustees meeting to see if any board members would be interested in volunteering in one of your teen programs.

- *Reach out to professional organizations.* Most professional fields have professional organizations. Check to see if there is a local chapter of organizations like the American Society of Mechanical Engineers or AIGA. When you find professional organizations in your area, ask if they would be willing to share information about your volunteer program with their membership.

- *Reach out to local businesses.* Many corporations encourage employees to volunteer in the community. Contact local businesses in industries that match your teens' interests and ask if they offer an employee volunteer program.

- *Reach out to schools and local universities.* Students can also be great volunteers. Check with the guidance department at your local high school or the career center at a local college. This can be a great way to advertise your volunteer opportunities to interested students. Many schools require students to complete community service before graduation. Find out if the schools in your area require community service. If so, see if the school would be willing to advertise the library's volunteer opportunities to students in need of community service hours.

Onboarding Your Volunteers

Consider formalizing your volunteer process. It is certainly worth the time that you will spend ensuring that volunteers will move smoothly through the application process and into their new role as a volunteer. Here are some things to consider:

- *Create a job description for your volunteers.* Once you have determined the goal of your volunteer program, take the time to create a volunteer description. A specific volunteer description can help you clarify a volunteer's role. You would want to make sure that you have this figured out before you begin recruiting volunteers. (See Appendix B for an example of a sample job description.)

- *Have volunteers complete an application.* Create an application for interested volunteers to complete. This enables you to collect a person's contact information, educational background, professional experience, and special skills. This is useful information to have when you are trying to match a volunteer to a particular program. For instance, if you know that a volunteer worked as an mechanical engineer, you can reach out to him or her if you are planning a robotics program for your teens.

- *Require volunteers to submit to a criminal background check.* A criminal background check can help you ensure that your teens are safe. Your public library or school likely already has a process in place for performing background checks on potential employees. Reach out to your human resources department or the person in your organization who handles the hiring process for new employees and find out if the process can be adapted for volunteers. Consider including a statement on the volunteer application that all volunteers are required to submit to a criminal background check.

- *Create a volunteer orientation.* Do your volunteers know and understand the purpose and goals of your volunteer program? What about your library's policies? Are volunteers expected to know how to operate specific technology or equipment in library programs? A formalized volunteer orientation should address these questions. Orientation can be done in-person, where a staff person walks volunteers through library policies and procedures and outlines volunteer expectations. (See Appendix B for an example of a new volunteer orientation outline.) If in-person orientation is not feasible for your library, you could also conduct a virtual orientation for volunteers. Create a document that you can e-mail to volunteers. If volunteers are getting the information online, be sure to follow up with an e-mail or a phone call. Ask the volunteer if he or she has any questions or would like clarification on the information that he or she has read.

- *Determine how volunteers will be scheduled.* Are volunteers being used for specific programs, or are volunteers working in the teen space during specific times? After you have determined how you are using your volunteers, you need to figure out how you will schedule the volunteers.

Working with Volunteers

Setting and Maintaining Expectations

Before you jump into working with volunteers, it is important to make sure that you have defined clear expectations. Creating and communicating expectations sets the program up for success. Before a volunteer's first library program, schedule some time to talk through the experience. This can be done over the phone or in person. Plan to discuss the following items with your volunteer:

- *Logistical information*: Let the volunteer know when he or she should arrive and where he or she should check in. Be sure to build in some extra time between the volunteer's arrival and the start of your program. This additional time will allow you to show the volunteer around the library, introduce him or her to other staff, and talk through the program.

- *Background information*: Give the volunteer some background information about the teen programs that your library offers. If you get the sense that the volunteer has not been to the library recently, make sure to paint an accurate picture of what he or she can expect in a library program. Some volunteers may have an outdated idea of libraries as quiet places. Other volunteers might think that a library program is like a classroom lesson. If programs are typically unstructured and happen right in the teen room, make sure that you communicate this information to your volunteers. You want to make sure that your volunteer does not walk into any surprises. If possible, consider inviting your volunteer to observe another library program so that he or she can see a program in action.

- *Program information*: Talk through the program with the volunteer. Explain what you have planned for the program and detail the tasks that you would like the volunteer to perform. Make sure that the volunteer understands what you would like him or her to do, and confirm that the volunteer is comfortable with the tasks. Share helpful planning materials with the volunteer before the program. These types of materials can include a program outline, YouTube videos, and websites with information about your activity. Program information should be sent to the volunteer at least several days before the program. While you cannot guarantee that the volunteer will look over the information before the program, you want to make sure that he or she at least has that option.

Engaging Volunteers

A person's time is precious. Because a volunteer is donating his or her time to help your teens and your library, you want to do as much as you can to ensure that the volunteer has a positive and rewarding experience. Communicating expectations is a great first step. Here are some other things that you should do to make sure that your volunteers feel welcome and appreciated:

- *Let other staff know that a volunteer is coming.* A volunteer should not be met with a blank stare when he or she checks in at the information desk. Make sure that all staff know that a volunteer is coming to the library to help out at a program.

- *Take the time to orient volunteers to your library.* Walk volunteers around the library and introduce them to staff.

- *Introduce volunteers to the teens.* Make sure that volunteers have an opportunity to introduce themselves during the program. If possible, let the volunteer share a bit about his or her background with your teens. This can be a fantastic way to connect a learning experience with possible career opportunities. Teens may learn about jobs or career paths that they did not know existed.

- *Do not assume that all volunteers will feel comfortable jumping right into a program.* Some volunteers will jump right in, and others might defer to you to invite them to participate. If you notice that your volunteer is hanging back during a program, check in with them. Make sure that they understand the activity and ask them if they feel comfortable assisting with the tasks.

- *Ask your volunteers for feedback.* It is so important to collect feedback from your volunteers after a program. Ask for feedback about both their experience volunteering and the program itself. Getting feedback gives you an opportunity to improve the program for both the teens and the volunteers. Ask volunteers for suggestions on how the program can be improved in the future. You should also ask them if the volunteer experience matched their expectations. If it did not, find out what could have been done to make their experience more positive.

- *Thank your volunteers for their time.* Make sure that you thank your volunteers for their help. Planning volunteer appreciation events on an annual or semiannual basis is another way to show your volunteers how much your value their time and commitment to your youth and your library.

Connected Learning in Action: Cuyahoga County Public Library's STEAM Volunteer Program

In 2014, the newly formed Literacy & Learning Division at Cuyahoga County Public Library (CCPL) embarked on a plan to shift all teen programs to a connected learning model. The Literacy & Learning Division consisted of the following departments: Adult Programming, Youth Programming, Youth Literacy & Outreach, and Information & Technology Literacy (ITL). Since the ITL department had piloted many youth initiatives involving technology, the department formed an action group of teen librarians from five locations throughout the library system to develop content for a staff in-service and pilot programming ideas to introduce CCPL's teen staff to connected learning. The action group was intentionally stacked with ringers. The five teen librarians had consistently shown an interest in developing innovative programming for youth and were also either comfortable with technology or willing to learn something new. All of the group members were also already engaging in programs that could fall somewhere on the connected learning spectrum. The group met in February 2014 to define mission and goals, determining how they would split up the topics they defined as most important to create program guide resources that other CCPL teen staff could use as a starting point for their connected learning programs.

Concurrent to the action group beginning its work, CCPL applied for a grant in February 2014 to fund connected learning through the Encore program of the Cleveland Foundation. CCPL received word that the grant had been awarded, in April 2014. The Encore Community Connects program jump started CCPL's pilot. As a part of the Encore program, the Cleveland Foundation grant focused on providing enriching experiences for people in their encore years—beyond retirement but looking to give back. Through the grant, CCPL was given the opportunity to craft a volunteer program and orientation process for this demographic that previously had not existed. The STEAM (science, technology, engineering, arts, and math) volunteers, as they came to be known, would be recruited to function as mentors in connected learning programs beginning with the pilot branches.

STEAM COORDINATORS

CCPL used some of the Encore Community Connects grant funds to hire three STEAM coordinators as contract employees. All three coordinators were retired professionals from varied backgrounds: one of the coordinators was a retired architect, one was a former middle school teacher and technology coach, and one was a grant writer with a master's degree in adult education. The STEAM coordinators' role was to work with ITL, the pilot branch staff, and teens to get a sense of the program needs and design a volunteer recruiting and orientation program.

To say that CCPL was lucky to receive the grant and the opportunity to hire the coordinators would be an understatement. The STEAMs, as they affectionately became known, came to function as mentors, not only to the teens in programs but to branch staff. They served an important role for ITL too. Not only did the STEAMs give ITL staff additional knowledge of how programs were working out in the branches but they also helped clarify areas where staff education was needed, including engaging volunteers and customer service with teens.

VOLUNTEER PROCESS CREATION AND TESTING

CCPL is a unionized library. Until recently, volunteers were a very tricky proposition. While volunteers were used in the system's homework centers and youth literacy programs, using them in other capacities was viewed as taking union work from professional staff and considered off-limits. Before embarking on the connected learning pilot, the Literacy & Learning Division worked closely with CCPL's union to ensure that the process being created for the STEAM volunteers and the volunteer job description was approved by all stakeholders. The parties agreed upon a volunteer job description that emphasized the contributions that volunteers make that are complementary to staff work. This also helped define the role that staff play in program creation and facilitation. The process was a positive exercise for all entities and provided clarification of roles on multiple levels. The STEAM coordinators worked with ITL to document all of the challenges they identified as mentors in CCPL's connected learning programs and outlined all of the details that they felt were beneficial for volunteers to know. Through the process, the STEAMs served as advocates for teens, library staff, and volunteers, guiding the process to a point where there was a working draft of a volunteer orientation and process.

MENTORS

Part of the connection in connected learning is linking youth with mentors who will support and encourage their growth. At CCPL, these mentors are STEAM volunteers. Volunteers were not required to have a technology background; the main requirement was an interest in working with teens. There were challenges along the way. Not every volunteer was suited to working with youth or in a library. CCPL quickly learned that it is imperative that staff communicate program expectations to volunteers. There were several situations where volunteers thought that they would lead programs on their own. There were also instances where volunteers brought their own materials and supplies to programs and then asked that they be reimbursed. While these examples were difficult or awkward at the time, they ultimately served as a great learning experience because they identified topics that needed to be included in volunteer procedures. Based on these experiences, the STEAM coordinators included language in CCPL's volunteer orientation about who facilitates teen programs (staff, not volunteers) and who provides materials and supplies for programs.

The resulting process yielded a committed and devoted group of volunteers. It took time to develop this process, and CCPL did lose volunteers who were too impatient to wait while the process was created. In the end, the conclusion at CCPL was that the volunteers who were the right fit for working with youth in library programs were the ones who waited through the process and remained engaged.

STEAM VOLUNTEER ADVISORY COUNCIL

The STEAM coordinators were originally hired as contract employees who would work for the duration of the grant from October 2014 to March 2016. During these 17 months, the STEAM coordinators did an incredible amount of work to create and implement CCPL's STEAM volunteer program. CCPL was lucky enough to renew the Cleveland Foundation grant for a second year. The additional time allowed CCPL to extend the STEAM coordinators' contract for an additional 12 months. The goal of the STEAM coordinators' second contract was to ensure the sustainability of the program. As ITL staff and the STEAM coordinators were continuing to polish the volunteer process and procedures, they determined that to truly engage volunteers, it would be beneficial to develop a volunteer advisory council that would assist in performance improvement for the overall volunteer process. That group would provide a valuable bridge for the system once the STEAM coordinators' contract ended.

One of the STEAM coordinators' most important functions was to share with ITL staff how the volunteer program was working at the branches. The STEAM Volunteer Advisory Council helped continue this work. CCPL's STEAM Volunteer Advisory Council is comprised of the following people:

- Current STEAM volunteers
- Rotation of teen librarians (each teen librarian attends one meeting per year)
- CCPL's volunteer coordinator
- ITL staff

The group meets monthly to discuss CCPL's STEAM volunteer program. Current volunteers and the rotating teen librarian share their experiences and identify ongoing issues or challenges that need to be addressed. The volunteers and librarians also report to ITL staff when additional communication or education is needed. The group has proved to be invaluable to CCPL's STEAM volunteer program.

BACKSLIDING AND CONTINUED PROCESS IMPROVEMENT

For CCPL, the process has been a continuous one. There is always an opportunity to refresh programming or to reevaluate the process. Staff changes necessitate additional training; and as staff and teen personalities and interests shift at branches, sometimes a fresh look is necessary. Because a robust and continued volunteer program is also new for CCPL, it is necessary to review the process and make updates as necessary. Revisiting the mission and basic outcomes of the program is an effective way to remind staff of the goals and desired results for our community. It is also a great opportunity to celebrate success and recognize where the program is really working and the staff and teens that make it all possible.

The process of integrating the connected learning model into youth programming has shown its value with increased youth engagement and additional opportunities for advocacy and partnerships. There will always be work to do and a process to review for CCPL. A focus on facilitation and the process of effectively facilitating youth programs is also a continuous challenge. That shift in mind-set will take the longest for staff to comfortably adopt. Technology will also need to be refreshed at some point. Funding is easier to secure for the initial technology purchase, and it is more challenging to find dollars to update or replace equipment. The ongoing work remains, but the opportunity to integrate connected learning and new methods of youth engagement has been well worth the work for Cuyahoga County Public Library.

WHEN VOLUNTEERS ARE NOT AN OPTION

Traditional volunteers are not always an option. Your public library or school may prohibit volunteers from assisting in youth programs or classes for a number of reasons. If this is your reality, how can you still provide your teens with the benefit of mentors without turning to outside experts for help? Are you and your teens out of luck? Absolutely not!

Look to Your Teens

Age is not necessarily an indicator of a person's level of knowledge of a subject. Do you have teens at your library who are really passionate about something? (The answer is yes!) Teens who are passionate about a topic are likely to have deep knowledge on that subject because they are spending the time to find and learn additional information and develop new skills. Find these teens and ask them if they would be willing to serve as mentors to other teens. Giving teens the ability to mentor their peers not only ensures that the teens in your library programs can work with subject experts but also enables you to create leadership opportunities for your teens.

Look to Your Colleagues

Earlier in this chapter, we suggested looking to your colleagues to serve as volunteers in programs. If your public library or school library does not allow outside volunteers in youth programs, can you find a workaround by turning to current employees? Please know that we are in no way suggesting that you sidestep a library policy. Before moving forward with this plan, make sure you clear this idea with your manager or supervisor.

Virtual Volunteers

If the experts cannot come to your teens, can you bring your teens to the experts? One of the pillars of the connected learning model is the use of technology in learning. A huge advantage to our connected world is that teens today are not limited to the physical books and people that they interact with in real life. Teens can use digital tools to find online resources and communities of experts to connect with regardless of location. You can do the same thing and look for online communities and experts for your teens. Reach out to the experts whom you connect with and see if anyone would be willing to join a program via Skype or FaceTime. This way you can still provide teens with the opportunity to connect with a subject expert. If anything, you may also find that you can foster a richer learning experience since you can reach beyond your local community for a virtual volunteer.

Connected Learning in Action: Homer Public Library, Alaska, Uses Skype to Connect Teens to App Developers

Homer Public Library's youth service librarian, Claudia Haines, is actively working to draw connections for the teens in her Alaskan community and the tech industry. A recipient of a grant through the American Library Association's Libraries Ready to Code initiative, the Homer Public Library is offering programs that support computational thinking for teens aged 11–14. Since the local schools do not teach computer science, the Homer Public Library is offering regular coding programs. To make the connection personal, Claudia Haines is reaching out to people with Alaskan roots who work in various technology fields. During the regularly scheduled library programs, teens can Skype with Alaskan-born app developers and programmers to learn about their education and career path (Haines, personal interview, 2017).

SUMMARY

Library staff do not need to be experts on a variety of topics to support connected learning. Instead, staff should begin to think of themselves as facilitators who connect teens to resources and tools that can expand their knowledge on subjects. These resources can include people, namely, volunteers, who can work with library staff to support connected learning programs.

ACTION STEPS

1. Find one professional development opportunity that you can participate in to support your role as a lifelong learner. Check with your state and regional chapters of the American Library Association for local conferences. Visit the websites of local youth work organizations to see if they offer trainings. Attend a webinar sponsored by YALSA or another professional organization.

2. Make a list of organizations, businesses, or people that you could contact about volunteer opportunities.

3. Talk to your teens and find out if any of them are interested in helping out with teen programs or facilitating programs on their own.

6

◇ ◇ ◇

PLANNING THE PROGRAMS

The easiest way to support and foster connected learning in your library is through engaging and impactful programs. By offering programs on topics that your teens are interested in, you can connect them to resources, individuals, and communities, where they can learn more about those subjects. When you embrace the connected learning framework, you may need to rethink your approach to programming. This chapter will break down the steps to develop and facilitate programs, give you a variety of ideas and resources to develop your own programs, and provide you with a couple of complete program plans to get you started in your own library.

PROGRAMMING 101

Programming is a process with specific steps: preplanning, planning, marketing and promotion, execution, and reflection. Do not fall into the trap of spending all of your time focused on the activity or event. This can be easy to do when you are dealing with the realities of less staff and more work. Library staff at both public libraries and school libraries are used to wearing a million hats, juggling work at an information desk, and managing the day-to-day operations of a department or branch. Stay focused on the big picture. Use some of the following questions to help guide your process:

- What types of programs are you hoping to offer in your library or media center to support your teens' interests?
- Are your programs based on outcomes? If you are a school librarian, chances are high, but even public libraries have embraced outcome-based assessments now. By designing programs with measurable goals and outcomes, you can demonstrate the value and impact of your programs. This is extremely helpful when trying to generate support for your teen programs and when looking for grants.
- Can you plan programs and look for partners who will continue to move your teens' interests forward?
- Are you working with volunteers? If so, do the volunteers connect the programs to real-world, career connections for your teens?
- Are you creating a structure or a pathway for your programs so that teens can progressively increase their knowledge as they attend your programs?
- Are you capturing feedback from teens before and after programs?

1. Preplanning: Offer Programs That Reflect Your Teens' Interests

Step One is to offer programs that reflect teens' interests. Do not fall into the trap of planning programs that reflect your interests instead of the interests of your community. You might love video games, but if the teens in your community are not interested in gaming, do not plan a gaming tournament. Programs should also reflect the interests of your whole community, not just a segment of your teen population. As Mega Subramaniam notes in the paper, "Designing the Library of the Future for and with Teens: Librarians as the 'Connector' in Connected Learning,"

> Teen service librarians will need to design programs and services that appeal to every culture and every teen year-round, not only seasonally. Having poetry-related activities solely during National Poetry month or having programs that appeal or appreciate African American culture exclusively during Black History Month is no longer acceptable. (Subramaniam 2016)

How do you find out what your teens are interested in? Start by talking to your teens. Ask the teens who come into your library about their interests. If you see groups of teens working together on a project, playing video games together, or creating something, ask them about what they are doing. During these conversations, find out if the activities could work as library programs.

The teens who regularly come into your library are easy to engage because you actually see them. But what about the teens that are only occasional library users? These are teens that come in to grab a book or do some research for an assignment but do not actually attend library programs. An even bigger challenge are the teens in your community or school that do not use your library at all. How do you find out about this audience's interests? Start by making use of traditional methods:

- *Surveys.* Use a paper survey or electronic survey using a free tool like Survey Monkey (www.surveymonkey.com). Other nontraditional surveys like sticker surveys can also work to quickly gauge teen interests. To reach teens who do not come into the library, share the surveys on the library's social media platforms. You can also reach out to local organizations to see if they will share the surveys. If you work in a school, ask teachers to distribute the surveys to their classes. If you work in a public library, ask the school and/or places like the local community center to see if you can distribute surveys there. (See Teen Program Survey in Appendix B for an example.)
- *Focus groups.* Put together a focus group of teens that regularly use your library. Existing teen groups like a teen advisory board could also serve as a focus group.

While these methods have their benefits, you are still likely only capturing responses from your regular and occasional users. To reach nonusers, you need to cast a bigger net. If you are a public librarian, be sure to reach out to the librarians in the local middle school and high school. If you are a school librarian, reach out to the teen librarian at the local public library. Both public and school librarians should make contact with teachers, advisors, and coaches. Find out if teachers or advisors can distribute a survey for you—or better yet, find out if they would be willing to bring their class or student group to the library or if they would let you visit the classroom or regular meeting. Get face time with the teens you are not currently reaching. Use this opportunity to make connections with these teens and to sell them on the library's programs and resources. Contact other community organizations that have teen groups. You can also ask the group facilitators about their teens' interests and find out if there is an opportunity to partner on programs or events.

Know Your Community

Chances are your library is not the only place in your area that offers programs for teens. Make sure that you do a scan of your community before you begin planning programs. You want to make sure that you are not replicating the programs that other organizations already offer. Here is a list of the types of organizations to look for:

- 4-H clubs
- Boys and girls club
- Community centers
- City recreation department
- Local library
- Local schools
- Museums
- Religious organizations

It is also important to know the local organizations that work with youth when you are looking for community partners. Perhaps you can offer your services as a co-facilitator for future teen programs?

2. Planning: What Does Your Program Look Like?

Using the data you have collected from surveys and conversations with teens and other youth work professionals, zero in on a topic or two that you would like to focus on. Take this time to start thinking through how you could turn the idea into a teen program. Is this something that you or other library staff can facilitate? Would the program be more impactful if you looked for an outside expert or volunteer to facilitate the program? Sketch out the basic program plan and determine when you are going to hold the program. Check with other organizations in your community to make sure that the program does not conflict with any community events. Factors like school project deadlines, sporting events, and club meetings can impact the number of teens who are able to attend your program. After you have scheduled your program, come up with a title and description for the program so that you can promote it. Make sure that the title and description are clear and specific. Titles like *Teen Tuesdays!* are catchy, but they do not convey any information about the actual program. On the other hand, the title *Teen Tuesdays: Tie Dyed T-shirts* very clearly states what the teens will do during the program.

Finalize the plans for your program. Once you have finalized your plans, do a dry run of the activity on your own. If you are making something or doing a demo, you want to make sure that you try it out before the program. For instance, you could find a program plan for a seemingly easy craft program on a site like Pinterest, but when you try to execute the activity you may discover that the steps are not clear or the end result is not what is advertised. It is better to find out what works and what does not work before the actual program. If you test your activity or demo early, you will still have time to make any needed adjustments before your actual program.

3. Marketing and Promotion: Selling Your Program

Once you have planned a thoughtful and impactful program that speaks directly to the interests of the teens in your community, you need to get the word out. Do not assume just because you planned a great program that you will get a great turnout. Check Chapter 7 for details on how you can effectively market your programs to teens and parents in your community.

4. Program Execution

Have fun! Remember that you do not need to be the expert—you are facilitating the learning experience. Give teens a chance to enrich the program by adding their own experience and knowledge. If the program involves a group activity, you might want to consider adding an icebreaker. Not all of your participants necessarily know each other. Including an icebreaker can make things comfortable for the teens and set the tone for a more participatory program. At the very least, make sure that you start the program with introductions. Let the teens know who you are, have the teens introduce themselves, and introduce any volunteers or mentors helping during the program.

5. Reflection: What Worked? What Did Not Work?

Build time to reflect into the program. It can be something as simple as asking the teens for feedback. What did they think of the program? What would they change if it was offered again? Ask two simple questions: What worked? What did not work? You can also collect more structured feedback with a survey. Make the survey anonymous to make teens more comfortable sharing feedback. Also, after the program, take some time for your own reflection. Review the teens' feedback and then include your own thoughts. Ask yourself the same questions you asked the teens: What worked? What did not work? Think about your answers and use that feedback when planning future programs.

At the end of the day, your programming process may look dramatically different from a colleague's programming process. That is OK. As you work through the different steps of program planning, you will find the strategies that work best for you.

INFORMAL ON-THE-FLOOR PROGRAMS VERSUS TRADITIONAL PROGRAMS

When you think of library programs, what immediately comes to mind? Do you picture a librarian and a group of teens in a meeting room? While these types of traditional programs are a mainstay of teen programming, they do not (and should not!) need to be the only way to offer teen programs in your library. Moving teen programs from a meeting room to the teen space can be a game changer. Below are a few compelling reasons why you should consider offering programs right in the library's teen area:

- *You are removing barriers.* How many times have you felt like you were practically pulling teeth trying to convince your teens to leave the teen room to attend a program in a meeting room? Sometimes, even asking teens to walk to another side of a room can seem like you are asking too much. When you hold programs right in the teen space, you are bringing the activity right to your teens.

- *On-the-floor programs are a great way to engage your after-school crowd.* Do you have a large and enthusiastic after-school crowd? Regularly providing programs right in the teen space is another way to positively direct teens. Sure, the teen room is absolutely about giving teens a space to hang out with friends, but when you start to facilitate programs in that space too, you are providing your teens with more options and opportunities.

- *On-the-floor programs allow teens to observe an activity before agreeing to participate.* As mentioned in Chapter 3, part of connected learning is allowing teens to lurk on the periphery of an activity. When you offer programs in the teen room, you are giving teens the opportunity to see what something is all about before they commit to joining in.

- *On-the-floor programs allow you to reach more teens.* Not all teens are interested in attending library programs. Teens taking part in activities and programs in the teen room may not even realize that they are attending a library program. This is absolutely OK. It is not important that teens know that they are at a program. It is important that teens are getting an opportunity to engage with others and to participate in an activity.

- *On-the-floor programs give you a chance to talk with your teens about their interests.* Some teens might feel like they are being put on the spot if you ask them about their interests. Instead of forcing a conversation, you can change the dynamic and create more natural opportunities to talk with your teens during an on-the-floor program. This is a chance to ask teens about what they are working on and have them share their knowledge too.

- *On-the-floor programs drive home the point that learning happens everywhere.* Libraries are informal learning spaces. When you are offering programs in the teen room, you are providing more learning opportunities for your teens.

- *On-the-floor programs are an easy way to showcase a transformed library.* This one is more for other library staff and customers than for teens. Today's libraries are about creating valuable experiences for all customers. When adults see a group of teens working together to use a green screen or program a robot, it provides an opportunity to point to a specific learning activity.

Once you are sold on the idea of offering informal on-the-floor programs, it is time to identify the right program to try out in that space. While many programs can be adapted to an on-the-floor environment, some will translate better than others.

Sample On-the-Floor Program:
Stop Motion Animation

Not every program works as an informal program that can be facilitated right in the library's teen space. When planning an on-the-floor program, choose an activity that can be kept simple but can also become more complex. Stop motion animation is a great example. It does not take much explanation and, depending on interest, a teen could create a movie in a matter of minutes or really dive into the activity and spend an hour creating a movie.

Objective: Introduce participants to basic principles of stop motion animation.

EQUIPMENT

- Tablet or smart phone with a stop motion animation app. The app Stop Motion Studio by Cateater, LLC works well. Free and paid versions are available for both iOS and Android platforms.

SUGGESTED MATERIALS
- LEGO bricks
- Paper
- Markers
- Dry erase board with markers
- Small toys (e.g., animals, action figures)
- Play-Doh

STEP ONE: PROVIDE A QUICK INTRODUCTION

Informal on-the-floor programs need to be simple enough that you can quickly and effectively explain the activity to teens. Stop motion animation works well because you can use a short video to explain the concept to teens. Either make your own quick video before the program to show teens as you introduce the activity or look for a video on YouTube. Try to find a video that is about 30–45 seconds long. The video does not need to go into the specifics of stop motion animation; it just needs to illustrate what a stop motion animation video looks like.

STEP TWO: PROVIDE MATERIALS AND EQUIPMENT

- Give the teens a tablet with the app loaded on the device. If you do not have tablets, invite teens with a smart phone to install a free app on their device. Encourage teens to work in pairs or small groups so that even teens without a device can participate in the activity.
- Set out a variety of the suggested materials for teens to use to make movies.

STEP THREE: PROVIDE A BRIEF OVERVIEW ON HOW TO USE THE APP

Instruct teens to open the app and walk them through how they can make their own stop motion movie. Set up a frame, capture a picture, make a small adjustment, capture a picture, and so on.

You may have some teens who will work on the movie only for a couple of minutes before they are ready to do something else. Remember, this is OK! The point of an informal on-the-floor program is simply to introduce a concept or technology to teens. Some teens will not be interested in moving beyond the basics.

STEP FOUR: HAVE EXTENSIONS READY FOR INTERESTED TEENS

While some teens will be interested only in the basics, an on-the-floor program might spark an interest in other teens who want to explore the topic further. Have ideas or extension activities ready to continue to challenge these teens. Here are a couple of examples that could work well for stop motion animation:

- Retold fairy tale challenge: Challenge teens to create a stop motion movie version of a popular fairy tale. Grab some picture books from the children's collection to use as inspiration.
- Introduce storyboarding: Find blank storyboard worksheets and challenge teens to plan and execute a more complex story.

STEP FIVE: REFLECTION

After the on-the-floor program, take the time to reflect on how the program worked. Were teens interested in learning about stop motion animation? When you were talking with teens who participated in the activity, did they seem interested in future programs? If so, think about if and how you could offer a more traditional animation program that could include additional concepts to continue to develop the knowledge and skills of your teens.

When planning an on-the-floor program, organization, simplicity, and flexibility are key. Teen librarians are already used to wearing multiple hats and shifting gears at a moment's notice. This skill can come in handy when facilitating an on-the-floor program. Understand and be OK with the fact that teens will likely float in and out of the activity. Designating a specific space in the teen area or school library is helpful, but remember that you will still have some teens who will only stay for a couple of minutes, some who show up late, and others who might stay for the entire program. This is not a reflection on you or on the program.

On-the-floor programs are a great way to introduce teens to new topics. When you are designing your program, make sure that you find a couple of resources that you can share with teens who want to pursue and dig deeper on their own. This can be as simple as a website, app recommendations, or YouTube tutorials on the topic. You can also use your on-the-floor program as a teaser for a more in-depth traditional program. After all, this is what connected learning is all about!

SAMPLE PROGRAMS

There are so many different programs that you can offer to support connected learning. The fact that it is so open ended can be overwhelming. We have selected three programs that can be easily adapted to suit the needs of a variety of libraries and teen audiences. These programs are budget friendly and do not require any specialized equipment. We will also include ways that you can add to the experience with additional tools or equipment, but it is not necessary to have this type of equipment to offer these impactful programs. Below is a quick overview of the three sample programs we have included. The detailed program curriculums for each program is included on the subsequent pages.

- *Chain reaction machine challenge.* A chain reaction machine challenge is a fantastic way to build teamwork and STEM skills in your teens. Depending on the types of materials and tools you are using, finding volunteers with design, construction, and/ or engineering experience can be a plus. Of course, this isn't required.

- *Paper circuits program.* Paper circuits like a light up greeting card are a good hands-on, entry level making program. Because a paper circuits program combines art and electronics, this can be a great gateway program for staff that are uncomfortable with facilitating making programs.

- *Take apart tech program.* Teens have an opportunity to learn how technology works by taking broken electronics and toys apart. Because the program can be done with screwdrivers and safety glasses, it is a great program to use when you are easing staff into using tools in programs.

CHAIN REACTION MACHINE CHALLENGE

Program Description: Teens will build a series of simple machines like pulleys and levers that are linked together. The action of one simple machine will trigger the next machine in a chain reaction. Ultimately, the machine will complete a specific simple everyday task or activity.

Audience age: This program is intended for children and teens in grades 5–12.

Number of participants: 12–15 participants.

Program duration: 2 hours.

Objective: Participants will work together to construct a chain reaction machine out of common household materials. Participants will build teamwork and critical thinking skills as they work together to design and build a machine that solves a challenge. Participants will use imagination and creativity to create their own design. Participants will also learn about cause and effect and how to apply basic physics concepts by constructing simple machines.

Examples of challenges: There are limitless possibilities for a chain reaction challenge. You can come up with your own original idea, or you can ask your group of teens to supply the challenge idea. Below are some additional ideas if you are looking for a place to begin:

- Pop a balloon
- Close a book or open a book
- Turn lights on or turn lights off
- Drop an object or pick up an object

Materials: You will need hardware (e.g., nails and screws), connection materials (e.g., glue and tape), and an assortment of other objects and materials—anything from wind-up toys to wood boards. The items that you select will dictate the type of hardware, connection materials, and tools you use. For instance, if you are using wood, you would want to make sure you have a hammer and a saw. Try to get a variety of materials. The greater the assortment of materials you are using, the more opportunities for creativity. Here is a list of suggested materials to get you started:

Hardware:

- Hooks
- Nails
- Pushpins
- Screws
- Springs
- Washers

Connection materials:

- Binder clips
- Craft wire
- Fishing line
- Glue (white craft glue, wood glue, hot glue)
- Magnets
- Nylon string
- Paper clips
- Pipe cleaner
- Rubber bands
- Tape (masking tape, transparent tape, duct tape)
- Twine
- Yarn
- Zip ties

Objects and materials:

- Balloons
- Boxes
- Bubble wrap

- Cardboard
- Craft sticks
- Clothes pins
- Cups (Dixie cups, plastic solo cups)
- Deck of cards
- Discarded library materials (books, CDs, DVDs, magazines, newspapers)
- Dominoes
- Egg cartons
- Funnel
- Marbles
- Markers
- Metal cans
- Paint stirrers
- Paper
- Paper towel tubes
- Pencils
- Ping Pong balls
- Plastic bottles and containers
- Plastic silverware
- Straws
- Toys (wind-up toys, matchbox cars, etc.)
- Wire hangers
- Wood
- Wood skewers

Tools: The tools you use for the program will be dictated by the materials you choose. Here is a list of suggested tools:

- Clamps
- Glue gun
- Extension cords
- Hammers
- Hand saw
- Level
- Pliers

- Power drill
- Rulers
- Scissors
- Screwdrivers
- Tape measure
- Utility knife
- Wire cutter
- Wrench

Safety equipment: If you are using tools in the program, you need to have proper safety equipment for the teens. Safety equipment may include the following:

- Safety glasses
- Gloves

Program Steps

Step One: Welcome and Introductions

Welcome the teens to the program, and introduce yourself. Ask the teens to introduce themselves. If you have any volunteers assisting you in the program, ask the volunteers to introduce themselves.

Step Two: Background Information and Discussion

A chain reaction machine is typically a collective machine that is made up of a series of simple machines. A simple machine is "any device that makes work easier" (COSI 2000). Each machine is linked so that the action of one machine sets off the action of the next machine. The simple machines use natural forces like gravity or force to move the action forward. For example, a person pushes a domino that sets off a whole line of dominoes. The dominoes are arranged so that the last one hits a ball that rolls down a ramp and falls into a plastic cup that triggers a pulley that sets off another action and so on.

Depending on the knowledge of the participants, you may need to talk more about simple machines. There are six types of simple machines:

- Wedge
- Wheel and axle

- Lever
- Inclined plane
- Screw
- Pulley

Step Three: Share Examples

Before your program, check YouTube for chain reaction videos that you can show as examples. Share the videos with the group. As you are showing the videos to the group, ask guiding questions to get them thinking and talking about the activity. Here are questions you can ask:

- How many steps are in that chain reaction machine?
- Does anyone see any simple machines in the chain reaction machine?
- What simple machines do you see?

Step Four: Review Safety Information

If you are using tools in the program, it is important that you take the time to review safety information. Make it clear to teens that they must use tools safely in order to participate in the program. Explain that anyone who does not abide by the safety rules will be asked to leave the program. The safety guidelines used in your program will depend on the materials and tools that you are using. Some guidelines could include the following:

- Any person operating power tools or hand tools must wear protective gear and dress appropriately.
- Safety glasses must be worn.
- Long hair must be tied back.
- Loose-fitting clothing should be tucked in.
- No neckties, jewelry, or dangling objects of any kind should be worn.

Step Five: Demonstrate Using Tools

After reviewing the safety guidelines for using tools, model the correct and appropriate way to use each tool.

Step Six: Introduce the Challenge

Now that the group understands and has talked about chain reaction machines, it is time to introduce the challenge. Explain to the group what action the machine should ultimately perform (e.g., pop a balloon, or turn off a light). Show the group the materials that they will have to build their machine. Let the group know how long they will have to design and build their machine. Every group's process is going to be different.

Depending on the number of participants you have in the program, you may want to split the teens into smaller groups. While the program can be run where everyone works in one group, it works best when the groups have three or four participants. If you have a larger group, you will likely spend more time trying to keep individual teens engaged and getting the whole group to function as team.

Step Seven: Brainstorming and Designing

Give the groups paper, pencils, and markers and ask them to start planning their machine. Encourage the group to get up and look at the materials. Be sure to spend a few minutes checking in with each group. During the check in, ask them about their design and ask them some guiding questions to help move their planning forward.

Every group's process is going to be different. Some groups will dive into the design and planning, while other groups will want to immediately get their hands on the tools. Planning is important, so make sure that every group spends at least some time planning.

Step Eight: Building and Testing

After the groups have planned their ideas, it is time for them to start building! Encourage the group to test throughout their building process. As the group is testing, they will be able to see how they might need to adjust their design.

Set an end time for the building and testing portion of the program. Encourage the group to keep track and manage their time. If groups have designs that are too complex, they may not be able to complete them.

There is going to be a great deal of trial and error during this program. Some groups will not finish their machine, and other groups will build a machine that cannot complete the task. That is OK. This is part of the process! Do not be discouraged—and more important—try not to let your teens become discouraged. Talk with your teens about the importance of failing and how every failure provides us with a greater opportunity to learn.

Step Nine: Share

Build time into the program for the groups to share and demonstrate their machines. If possible, invite parents and other staff members to check out the teens' creations. Ask the teens to talk about their process as part of their demonstration.

Step Ten: Reflection

As with every program you facilitate, make sure that you build in time for reflection. Get feedback from the teens on what they enjoyed about the program and what they did not enjoy about the program.

Additional Program Resources

- **Rube Goldberg, Inc.:** https://www.rubegoldberg.com/. Rube Goldberg machines are wacky chain reaction machines. Rube Goldberg, Inc. hosts annual Rube Goldberg competitions. The website has information about the real person, Rube Goldberg, as well as the information and rules about their contests.

Program extensions: Chain reaction programs can be as simple or as complex as you and your teens make them. If you would like to offer a program that can foster deeper learning, here are a couple of suggestions:

- *Physical and digital chain reaction machine.* Add a digital element to a chain reaction challenge. Teens can use MIT's Scratch program and the LEGO Education WeDo kit to create the digital element. A physical object like a ball would trigger one of the WeDo sensors that would run a program that the teens created in Scratch.
- *Turn your program into a camp.* Teens could easily spend hours designing and creating a chain reaction machine. If you have the time and the resources, consider expanding the activity into a week-long camp. Add additional materials and require the teens to add more steps to their final machine.

PAPER CIRCUITS PROGRAM

Program description: Create art that lights up! Learn about simple circuits and how you can incorporate them into your artwork.

Audience age: This program is intended for children and teens in grades 5–12.

Number of participants: 12–15 participants.

Program duration: 2 hours.

Objective: Participants will learn basic information about electricity and simple circuits. Participants will apply critical thinking skills as they work to design and create a piece of artwork that contains a circuit. Participants will use imagination and creativity to create their own design.

Materials

- Binder clip
- Cardstock
- Coin cell battery
- Conductive copper tape
- Conductive paint (optional)
- Construction paper
- LED
- Markers
- Pencils
- Transparent tape

Tools

- Scissors

Program Steps

Step One: Welcome and Introductions

Welcome the teens to the program, and introduce yourself. Ask the teens to introduce themselves. If you have any volunteers assisting you in the program, ask the volunteers to introduce themselves.

Step Two: Background Information and Discussion

At the beginning of the program, ask the teens if they are familiar with electricity and circuits. A simple circuit is a path that electrons flow from a power source to a device like a LED to make it work. For a simple circuit to work correctly, the path or loop needs to be closed. Ask the group if anyone can explain what a circuit is and how a circuit works.

During the conversation, be sure to talk through positive and negative connections. If you are using LEDs with leads, show the teens how they can identify which lead is positive and which lead is negative.

Step Three: Share Examples

Prior to the program, create some example paper circuits to share with the group.

Step Four: Demonstrate the Project

Before the teens design and create their own artwork with circuits, have them create simple circuits using templates. Prior to the program, look online for templates for simple circuits. The resources section below lists several websites that include tutorials and templates for circuits.

Give each participant a template and walk them through the process of creating a simple circuit. Model each step for the teens. Check in with the participants during each step to ensure that everyone is following along and understands how to create a working circuit.

Tip: When using copper tape to create circuits, try to use one piece of copper tape for the path. Sometimes, when you combine several pieces of copper tape, it can break the connection in the circuit.

Step Five: Creation

After everyone has an opportunity to create their own simple circuit using the template, teens can create their own artwork using circuits. Give the participants a variety of supplies to create their art, including card-stock, construction paper, and markers. Recommend that the teens use the simple circuit templates as a guide when creating their art.

Step Six: Share

Build time into the program for the groups to share their projects. If possible, invite parents and other staff members to check out the teens' creations.

Step Seven: Reflection

As with every program you facilitate, make sure that you build in time for reflection. Get feedback from the teens on what they enjoyed about the program and what they did not enjoy about the program.

Additional program resources: There are many available online resources for paper circuits programs. Some include the following:

- **Adafruit:** https://www.adafruit.com/. Adafruit is a great place to start when you are ready to purchase supplies for your paper circuits program. You will be able to find supplies for all sorts of electronics and making programs. The Adafruit website also includes guides and tutorials for different projects.
- **Chibitronics projects:** https://chibitronics.com/projects/. Chibitronics makes and sells electronic stickers. The stickers can be great for a paper circuits program. The Chibitronics website also includes tutorials on different types of circuits (e.g., simple circuit, parallel circuit).
- **The Great Big Guide to Paper Circuits:** https://learn.sparkfun .com/tutorials/the-great-big-guide-to-paper-circuits. This is a tutorial for a paper circuit program from the SparkFun website.
- **High-low tech paper circuits with copper tape:** http://highlowtech .org/?p=2505. Print templates for different types of circuits, including simple circuit, circuit with switch, circuit with pull tab switch.
- **SparkFun**: https://www.sparkfun.com. Like Adafruit, SparkFun is a useful resource when you are looking for supplies for electronics and making programs. The SparkFun website also includes tutorials and lessons for a variety of maker projects.

Program extensions: You could enrich your paper circuits program in several ways. Some examples include the following:

- *Add additional circuits to the project.* If your program featured a simple circuit, you can add complexity by including additional circuits in the project. You could also challenge participants to figure out how to add a switch to their circuit.
- *Try a sound circuit.* Instead of making a circuit with LEDs, try to create a sound circuit. Be aware that you will need additional supplies and tools to create a sound circuit.

TAKE-APART TECH PROGRAM

Program description: Discover how technology works by taking broken electronics and toys apart with tools.

Audience age: This program is intended for children and teens in grades 5–12.

Number of participants: 12–15 participants.

Program duration: 90 minutes.

Objective: Participants will use hand tools to take apart old and broken toys and electronics. Participants will build critical thinking skills as they discover how technology and electronics work and how technology has evolved over time. Participants will also learn basic tool safety.

Materials: You will need broken electronics or toys that teens can take apart during the program. Not all electronics are safe to take apart. Items like televisions can hold a charge. Computers and cell phones can contain dangerous chemicals. Before your program, do some research to make sure that teens can safely take apart the items that you have selected for the program.

When you are ready to collect items for your program, check your library or school to see if there are any broken or outdated electronics that the system is going to recycle. You can also ask colleagues if they have any old or broken items that they want to donate for your program. If you are having difficulty getting enough items from your library and/or your colleagues, you could also go to a local Goodwill or thrift store to buy items. Here is a list of suggested materials to get you started:

- VCR
- DVD player
- Computer keyboard
- Remotes
- Landline phone
- Mechanical alarm clocks
- Electronic toys

Tools: The tools you use for the program will be dictated by the materials you choose. Here is a list of suggested tools:

- Hammers
- Screwdrivers—you will need slotted, phillips, and torx screwdrivers in multiple sizes
- Pliers

Safety equipment: Since you are using tools in the program, you need to have proper safety equipment for the teens. Safety equipment may include the following:

- Safety glasses
- Gloves

Program Steps

Step One: Welcome and Introductions

Welcome the teens to the program, and introduce yourself. Ask the teens to introduce themselves. If you have any volunteers assisting you in the program, ask the volunteers to introduce themselves.

Step Two: Background Information and Discussion

At the beginning of the program, ask the teens if they have ever tried to figure out how something works by taking it apart. Ask the teens to identify the items that are available to take apart and see if the teens know how the items were used. Depending on the items that you have to take apart, talk with the teens about technology and how it has evolved and advanced over time.

Step Three: Review Safety Information

Since you using tools in the program, it is important that you take the time to review safety information. Make it clear to teens that they must use tools safely in order to participate in the program. Explain that anyone who does not abide by the safety rules will be asked to leave the program. The safety guidelines used in your program will depend on the materials and tools that you are using. Some guidelines could include the following:

- Any person operating hand tools must wear protective gear and dress appropriately.
- Safety glasses must be worn.
- Long hair must be tied back.
- Loose-fitting clothing should be tucked in.
- No neckties, jewelry, or dangling objects of any kind should be worn.

Step Four: Demonstrate Using Tools

After reviewing the safety guidelines for using tools, model the correct and appropriate way to use each tool.

Step Five: Distribute Items and Tools

Have the teens select items to take apart. Distribute tools and safety glasses for the teens to use while taking apart the electronics. Encourage the teens to work together to take apart items and to share what they find with each other.

Step Six: Reflection

As with every program you facilitate, make sure that you build in time for reflection. Get feedback from the teens on what they enjoyed about the program and what they did not enjoy about the program.

Program extensions: A take-apart tech program is a relatively simple program with potentially high impact. You can further enrich your program by incorporating art. Here is one example:

- *Up-cycled art sculpture.* After teens have taken apart the items, have them use the various pieces to create an up-cycled art sculpture. Either the teens can create their own individual artwork or all of the participants can work together to create one art installation. If possible, display the finished artwork in the library.

SUMMARY

Creating impactful, interest-driven programs for teens is at the heart of connected learning. Use a combination of methods to determine the types of programs your teens are interested in, including conversations with teens, surveys, and on-the-floor programs. Before planning your teen programs, make sure that you are not replicating programs offered at other community organizations. Whenever possible, see if you can get out in the community to find and reach teens who do not regularly come into the library for programs.

ACTION STEPS

1. Conduct a scan of the organizations in your area that offer programs for teens. Create a list of the organizations. Visit the organizations' websites to familiarize yourself with their program offerings. Compare those programs with the programs that you facilitate at your library and identify any duplications.

2. Create and distribute a survey to gauge teen program interests.

3. Try an informal on-the-floor program with your teens.

7

◇ ◇ ◇

MARKETING AND PROMOTING
THE PROGRAM

As with any other library program, finding effective methods to promote your connected learning program is essential. Public perception of libraries is behind the times, and innovative library services are not an expectation. Keep in mind that building a new perception takes time. Changing the community's view of what you do will evolve over time and not all at once. It will take more than one advertisement or flyer to reach a new audience or to sell a new perception to your current audience. Plan to invest continued time and resources to change your image in your community. Be authentic to the organization that you were and are becoming. When your message works and customers seek out your services, ensure that the organization and programs that you are promoting are indeed what you are offering. Continue to demonstrate and promote your current role and the role of the organization that you desire to be and your image will change gradually.

The traditional view of the library outside our profession is not one of change and vibrant digital connections. That can be and is what libraries are becoming, but the public view of libraries often lags behind the actual change taking place. No one single message will reach everyone and have an impact. Finding and reaching parents is one thing, but reaching tweens and teens themselves is an ever-evolving dilemma. This chapter offers ideas for effective outreach methods and methods to keep the conversation going.

REACHING YOUR AUDIENCE

Reaching a youth audience can be challenging. They do not want flyers or email. They might respond to a text, but that means putting a system in place that will allow you to text marketing details to a youth audience. Many libraries also do not make a habit of collecting information from kids, so even if you have that system in place, you may not have the contact information to use it. You can try to use social media, but platforms are constantly changing and teens generally do not want the library on their social media accounts. When the adults appear, they move to something new. Let's face it: as much as your library is offering cool programs for teens, you are probably not cool enough to garner an invite to their social media groups.

Reaching Adults

Parents represent one way to forge a connection. Getting young people to a program offers the opportunity to connect personally. Parents are much more available through traditional marketing methods: flyers, website, email, and social media. You may have to overcome some additional obstacles with teens who don't want to initially be in your program if their parents have suggested it, but reaching parents to ensure that youth are there can be a good method to begin engagement. Parents are looking for enriching and interesting learning opportunities for their kids, and the library is already considered a resource. However, parents can be more likely to have a more traditional, and less innovative, view of what a library does. So, you have to educate the parents. This takes consistent messaging and reaching out to parents to ensure that they recognize the ongoing services and programs that the library offers. Changing perception and building a new image means that parents will look to the library first once they are convinced of the value (Potter 2013).

Educating Parents

Making sure that parents understand the benefits of connected learning programming can have benefits for connected learning and your library's teen programming as a whole. Parent awareness around the asset of library programming for teens is an added plus, with great benefits to be seen from parental understanding of the STEAM (science, technology, engineering, arts, and math) and enrichment programs offered for teens during out-of-school time.

- Show the tie to literacy
- Show the tie to school subjects
- Show the promise of engagement
- Show the benefits

Making a case means showing the unique benefits of offering connected learning programs in your library.

To a certain extent, demonstrating library innovation and enlisting support can also depend on making connections between new, innovative programs and literacy. There are many literacies that apply to connected learning: media literacy, invention literacy, even transliteracy. Whether you are talking about learning a new technology or tool, or absorbing and consuming factual information, these are areas that libraries are known for. The exact medium and method of acquisition may change, but these areas are still firmly within the library staff's expertise. Making that connection for customers can be essential. Do not just assume that they will see the connection and understand. Make sure that you demonstrate your library's evolving role in literacies of all types. This can be accomplished by adding talking points about new literacies to staff's program information to marketing materials and even to library brochures and promotional talks. All programming can be tied back to literacy of some sort.

Reaching Teens

Once teens are in your program, you have the ability to reach out and try to make more connections. Parents may be coming into the library for their own needs and can be more open to marketing messages while they are at the library. You'll want all hands on deck for this type of messaging. Sure, your floor staff can make a connection for parents when they are asking questions, but circulation staff can do it too. Prepare and engage all library staff, whatever their department or role, in spreading the word. The impact made by a conversation can be far more lasting than a brief advertisement or flyer. Staff have the ability to enter into a dialogue with patrons and tie library programs and services to customer needs. There is less guesswork and wondering if your customers are getting your message when you know that staff are helping get the word out. Also, make sure that staff are aware and supportive to meet the demand when it does come. There is nothing worse than finally engaging your audience only to encounter a negative customer service experience when staff are not supportive (Potter 2012). A great example of this is collaboration between local government and libraries to promote a service. Residents are told that they can come to the library to sign up for the service, touting the library's convenient hours and knowledgeable staff. When residents come to the library, they encounter a staff person who is unfamiliar with the service and unsupportive of libraries offering social services. The customer leaves the library more frustrated than before and could be vocal with their family and friends about the lack of assistance. Both the library and local government spent time and money to publicize the service and train staff, but one negative interaction can do an enormous amount of harm. Taking extra time to ensure that staff recognize the value, benefits, and need for services in the community can help prevent such scenarios. Ensuring that staff see real customers who will benefit is also a motivator. Finally, ensuring that you have a way to hold staff accountable for learning and providing excellent customer service is always a beneficial first step toward ensuring that all staff provide consistent and excellent service.

The Labs @ CLP, Carnegie Library of Pittsburgh, Pittsburgh, Pennsylvania

Staff at the Carnegie Library of Pittsburgh (CLP) recognized that there was a need to engage teens and support the vibrant teen community in their spaces. The library sought funding for a space dedicated to youth that would allow them to pursue their passions with the help of adult mentors. Luckily for CLP, they were seeking to transform their teen presence at just the right time. They were awarded an IMLS and MacArthur grant in 2013 for Learning Labs in Libraries, and out of the funding, the Labs @ CLP launched five labs in CLP branches.

The spaces sought to teach new tools and 21st-century skills, building digital literacy and engagement through learning. The spaces are heavily dependent on staff and mentors to make connections with local youth, encouraging pursuit of their interests. Though staff intensive, this has paid off: youth bloom in the space, engaging in projects and programs, creating a learning community among themselves and with their digital mentors. Like many digital learning spaces, the Labs @ CLP provide formal workshop programming and informal drop in. There is plenty of time for hanging out, messing around, and geeking out. After all, the best way to really deeply learn about a topic is to geek out over the possibilities.

The Labs @ CLP offer audio recording, video editing, gaming, 3D design and printing, robotics, and lots of opportunities for crafting. Youth are encouraged to explore their interests, not limited to the technology on hand, and take advantage of the staff and mentors available.

Reaching parents can also have a big impact in a school setting. Although teens are a captive audience at school, true engagement takes support from all sides. Also, because connected learning is an unfamiliar approach for many, it takes some support outside the regular school day. In a world where parents are now engaged in knowing and questioning how everything covered relates to the test or learning outcome, it is useful to provide them with clarity on the goals and benefits of the method. Few parents and educators are enthusiastic about the confines of teaching to a test during school time. When connected learning is integrated into the school day and throughout the curriculum, it adds richness and engagement to even the most basic of skills. Teaching necessary principles in a manner that does not scream rote memorization and supports organic rather than forced peer engagement could be incredibly beneficial. Imagine a school world where you are still learning what they need to learn but empowered to do it.

Keeping in mind the challenges of reaching out to youth, what can you do to promote programs and encourage engagement? Our first suggestion is to talk to your teens. Start a conversation. Find out their interests.

- What are they reading?
- Are they longtime customers?
- Do they need homework help?

Your personal connection and interest in their lives is the best way to gain teens' trust. Many libraries have teen groups that engage in volunteerism or programming help. These teens can serve as your test group if you survey their interests. Ask about the interests of their peers while you are at it. Have your existing teen base help you plan a program that seeks to engage more youth in the community. That will serve two purposes: bringing in more teens and building engagement and trust with existing youth. Once you have teens in the library, seeing other teens having fun and engaging with each other provides an excellent draw. Youth who were initially resistant to engage can be persuaded when they see their peers having fun.

Using your already engaged teens can work in other ways too. Trust and ownership for the process can be built by including teens in library marketing and promotion efforts. Allow teens to write a guest blog or social media post. Reach out for their input when searching for new platforms in which to invest. Utilize the same survey method to ask them how they would wish to be approached with information about new programs. So much of connected learning involves allowing teen voices to be heard and valued that encouraging them to engage in any part of the planning process can be a beneficial step toward building ownership. You are already asking them to form peer relationships with other teens; why not encourage them to reach out and help you engage those teens in the first place?

Technology can also assist you in your efforts to draw teens in. While simply stating that you are using iPads, tablets, or robots usually is not a draw on its own, promoting what you are doing with the technology can be. Tablets, smart phones, and lower-cost devices like Chromebooks mean that technology ownership is more accessible than ever before. Teens may not come to a program for the technology alone, but parents and youth alike can be pulled in by new, fun things to do with the technology. Activities like digital animation, video creation, game creation, and coding can be accomplished with an app, a few hours, and some creativity. Remember, parents are often looking for ways to reach their kids through and with technology, and youth will rarely turn down the opportunity to learn something new and fun. The technology itself is an afterthought; it is the way that it can be used to form connections that is the big draw.

RAISING AWARENESS

Once you have planned a thoughtful and impactful program that speaks directly to the interests of the teens in your community, you need to get the word out. Do not assume just because you planned a great program that you will get a great turnout. Take time to promote your program to the teens in your community. Here are some guidelines for your promotions:

- *Include the program in your library event calendar.* This is a no brainer. Every single library program should be listed on the library's event calendar, whether in print, on the website, or both.

- *Talk to teens and parents.* Do not assume that all of your library customers check the library's event calendar. You need to hand-sell your programs whenever possible. Talk to every teen in your teen space about you upcoming programs, and don't be afraid to show your enthusiasm. You never know what type of program will spark a teen's interest.

- *Talk to your colleagues.* All library staff should be aware of upcoming library programs and events. Share your upcoming program plans with colleagues so that they can hand-sell programs to customers. Return the favor and promote other department programs. It is up to all library staff to connect customers with information, resources, and programs.

- *Reach out to community organizations that work with youth.* Send an email with upcoming library programs to local community groups. If the program aligns with a specific group's interests, invite the organization to bring their youth group to your program.

- *Reach out to local schools or the local public library.* If you work in a public library, reach out to the local middle schools and high schools to promote the program. If you work in a school, reach out to the local public library to promote the program.

- *Promote programs on your library's social media platforms.* Use the library's social media platforms, such as Facebook and Twitter, to promote your programs.

- *Promote programs in local newspapers and on community calendars.* Send a press release to your local newspaper. Look for online community event calendars where you can submit program information.

The more you promote the program, the more likely you will get a good turnout. If your program requires registration, make reminder phone calls or send reminder emails or texts a day or two before the program. If the program does not require registration, let your teens know about the upcoming program during one of your daily conversations.

After all of your best efforts, there is still the possibility that you will have planned and promoted a program as much as humanly possible and have a low turnout. Do not be discouraged. It can take time to build an audience around a subject, especially if you are trying something new. Make a couple of adjustments and try to offer the program again. A minor change like switching the day of the week from Tuesday to Wednesday could make all the difference.

Raising Staff Awareness

Even though they work for the same library or system, you may need to do some work to ensure that staff are aware of your connected learning program and events. While it may seem like all staff would be aware of things happening in the building where they work, this is often not the case. Taking a little extra time to share information and talking points about your connected learning program can be very helpful in encouraging staff to spread the word. You cannot be everywhere at once, but sharing the following information will help other staff act as very effective surrogates when it comes to informing the public about your program and events.

- Program name and purpose
- Intended benefits and outcomes
- Possible audience
- Upcoming events, including regular events if those are applicable

Making Connections at BOOMbox, Skokie Public Library, Skokie, Illinois

In 2009, the Skokie Public Library sought to address needs in the community by creating a digital media lab. The lab immediately saw use from all ages of the community and was by all measures a success. In 2014, the library staff saw that despite the success of the digital media labs, there was a need for experiential, hands-on STEAM learning in the community; they got to work and the BOOMbox was born.

The BOOMbox seeks to facilitate learning as a state of mind in the community. This starts with staff who have an early opportunity to try the equipment and activities available in each theme rotation. Early access seeks to boost staff buy-in and encourage engagement with community participants. Mentors in the space are mainly high school students with an interest in facilitating learning around STEAM topics and an aptitude for technology. The BOOMbox also works with one Dominican University intern. Data is collected in the form of surveys and observational accounts to understand the impact of each theme and the programming offered.

In addition to BOOMbox and the digital media labs, Skokie offers 3D printing by submission, device loans of equipment for digital creation, productivity, entertainment, and learning. They also host programming and discussion facilitated through their Civic Lab, specifically designed to provide discourse and resources around topics of current interest. Lively and participatory youth spaces can be found in the Civic Lab. Learners of all ages can find their niche at Skokie's library (https://skokielibrary.info/blog/boombox/).

Raising Community Awareness

Raising community awareness for your connected learning programming is a continuous process. In order to successfully raise community awareness, you need to identify local organizations that could be your advocates as you seek partners.

- Who has a similar mission?
- Who else in your community reaches out to engage youth?

Even in a small community, everyone has their role to play. Resources are scarce, and it is valuable to create a clear vision of who you are and what your institution stands for. Community organizations often become concerned that libraries are competing for similar funding and audience. Ensuring that your goals and role are clear can create bonds that align programs and clarify the differences in organizational purpose. Reach out to other groups that work with teens: recreation centers, other libraries, schools and teachers, PTA groups, parent groups, and local tech groups. These groups are not only potential partners and advocates but also excellent venues to recruit volunteers.

It is even possible that other community organizations will want to partner and help you create a more robust connected learning program. Local tech groups can help develop content and programs. Local parent groups may volunteer or share their own professional expertise. Other libraries or schools may have staff with different interests who are willing to share their knowledge in exchange for a program offered at their library or school. Even if they do not choose to partner, reaching out to raise awareness will enable you to ensure that you are not duplicating services.

FINDING PARTNERS

You may already have a good idea of who would be a complementary partner in your connected learning endeavors. If this is not the case, organizations that you already partner with make a great starting point. Most libraries partner with schools, parent groups, scout troops, local agencies, or extension offices. Seek out organizations that relate to teens, technology, or civic education in your community. These organizations should see the value of a resilient and engaged youth quickly. If you are currently working with organizations that program for youth, reach out to them to discuss integrating connected learning principles into their programs. If you have engaged library volunteers at any age, seek out their interest in mentoring youth or sharing their talents. Local businesses, retiree groups, or social service agencies are also possible sources. Also look to museums, recreation centers, and, of course, schools, for partners with like missions. Libraries often have a wide reach and an ability to spread a complimentary message. Just as libraries continuously look at how they can reach the elusive nonlibrary user, other local agencies are looking for ways to reach the community and share their message. Even schools that may reach most families look for methods to reach seniors and members of the community without children. Schools that adequately reach families in the community still need to reach seniors and community residents without children. Their support during a school levy is dependent upon an understanding of the mission and benefits of programming and services. Sharing a like message is a great benefit to promote. So too is the ability to explore a collection or exhibit from a local museum or an historical society. Libraries are very accessible and that accessibility often attracts audiences that may shy away from exploring other local organizations. There are numerous possibilities for shared benefits; you may just need to use a little creativity to uncover them.

Engagement at Studio NPL, Nashville Public Library

Nashville is known for a wealth of talent. Studio NPL facilities engage part-time instructors and partners, taking advantage of the wealth of music professionals in the Nashville area. Instructors and mentors bring their talents to share but are also trained to cultivate hanging out, messing around, and geeking out. The program also has connections to Vanderbilt University; Southern Word, a local organization committed to youth voice through literary and presentation skills; and community organizations, increasing potential for youth to gain valuable knowledge and experience with professional groups in the Nashville area.

The majority of Studio NPL youth come from underserved areas in and around Nashville. The Nashville Public Library actively works to recruit youth participants who may lack other opportunities to engage their peers and professionals in the community. Youth are encouraged to share their true selves through art, encouraging genuine engagement with each other and adult mentors (nplf.org).

Don't be discouraged if you have some negative reactions along the way. Partner organizations often have preconceptions and are accustomed to the cautious culture of libraries. Just like marketing to your customers, the process of finding the right partners can take time. Relating the work that you are trying to do to a potential partner's missions and goals will help you shift the image of the work that the library does in the community. Aligning missions and process can be complicated, but continuing to advocate for your connected learning program in your community and share your experiences will not only hone your advocacy skills but also help you clarify your true partnership needs. Continue to seek support in your community and be a champion on your connected learning program's success and your passion will attract those with like motivation.

It is no secret that it can be a challenge to reach teens with library services. There is no one-size-fits-all solution but a combination of outreach to community groups, promotion targeting parents, knowledgeable staff, and engaging teens to draw in their friends can create a very effective process for reaching the audience in your community.

SUMMARY

A thoughtful marketing and promotion effort is essential to the success of both your greater connected learning program and individual events. It is a process that involves some thought and outreach but with some work, it can produce enthusiastic parents, engaged teens, supportive colleagues, and local partner organizations. Following the steps laid out in this chapter can assist you as you develop your plans for outreach and building support.

ACTION STEPS

1. Create a plan to reach out to parents.
2. Empower your teen group to be a part of the marketing process.
3. Reach out to your schools. Find a supporter, maybe a media specialist, STEAM specialist, or arts teacher.
4. Find a community partner with like goals. Develop possible benefits from a partnership and reach out.

8

◇ ◇ ◇

ASSESS AND REFINE

A crucial aspect of any new learning movement is assessment to ensure that the change is indeed improving learning outcomes for youth. Connected learning represents a change in the design-of-libraries approach to teens, and programming and assessment is an essential element to ensuring that the program design is sound. Demonstrating value has moved beyond a heartwarming story or an impressive number of program attendees. You and your fellow library staff might feel a change in the library in the after-school hours. The atmosphere may have lightened, feeling less like a powder keg but pointing to reduced numbers of incidents involving teens proves the feeling. Funders and administrators want to see impacts in student engagement, increases in positive attitudes about library staff, and growth in knowledge.

Assessment can seem like a daunting task, but if you followed the steps of program creation outlined in our earlier chapters, most of the structure you need should already be in place. Early on, we suggested that you know your outcomes and tie them to areas of administrative concern. Your outcomes are what your assessment will measure. Ideally, you have been measuring these outcomes all along as your teens attended programs or you surveyed their interests. Surveying as you go along makes this process easier. If that is not feasible or has not occurred, choose times to survey or implement an assessment and put them in place now. Your outcomes form the structure and purpose for your program. Understand them and keep them in mind through everything that you do. Utilizing the backward design process should have also helped you define how you would measure your outcomes when you were developing your program. This measurement tool is what you will use now for assessment. Hint: This should have been explored when you created your outcomes.

It will be valuable for you to also be able to measure the true costs of the program. These were outlined when we discussed program design, but staff time, programmers, supplies, equipment, software including apps, space, marketing, and refreshments can all be cost elements. A comprehensive view and tally of these costs will demonstrate to your administration that you have a true sense of the overall impact and what it takes to run your program (see Program Cost Worksheet in Appendix B).

Whether you choose a formal assessor or choose to do the assessment on your own is a matter of choice and budget. Many systems do not have a budget for formal assessment, and grants do not always cover them. Formal assessments are a wonderful and impartial opportunity when you can secure one. If you believe that it will be challenging for staff to be impartial and to assess a program on their own, you can seek local organizations or institutions of higher education that may provide interns or graduate assistants to do the work in a project capacity. This is often a great opportunity to engage a formal assessment at a reduced cost. If you believe that staff can objectively look at the data collected and make modifications to the program, surveys are a great way to evaluate the program in house. Make sure to survey your teens, staff, and volunteers in the process. They should all provide feedback about what is working and what could be improved and sometimes that results are surprising.

Be able to measure the toll on staff too. Many of the ideas that we suggest here push staff outside their comfort zones. That can be exhausting. Rotating staff not only increases the opportunity for you to inject new ideas into the program but also allows new staff to share their passions and expertise, connecting with your teens. This can prevent burnout and keep staff engaged longer. Through pioneering programs, like YOUmedia, we are beginning to understand how essential staff engagement is to a connected learning program and rotating staff can help share the weight of the work. This is also an excellent opportunity to keep learning fresh among staff. Comfort with technology depends on fresh and frequent use, and anxiety is quick to reemerge when too much time passes. Rotating staff through programs helps them reconnect with both teens and tech, leading to increased knowledge and comfort.

Formal Evaluation of YOUmedia

A study of the Chicago Public Library's YOUmedia space by the University of Chicago Consortium on Chicago School Research found that many of the YOUmedia outcomes had been achieved. Youth who were deeply involved in the creation of media and who chose to fully geek out with tools reported that they felt supported by the adults and mentors and had increased digital skills. They also felt that they had increased their academic abilities and gave their experience at YOUmedia credit for improving their communication skills. The study clearly showed the success achieved in the space but also that it takes a lot of work. Engagement with teens can be hard and takes concerted effort from adult staff and mentors. Youth in the space were reluctant to engage on their own and often had to be persuaded by staff to try a program or technology. Adults in the space were key to connecting youth and their interests, making the presence of mentors critically important.

Managing and maintaining a digital learning space can also be complicated. YOUmedia staff saw availability of resources and technology as an ongoing challenge. The nature and pace of technology also required a very adaptive space and staff to remain current. Those issues can lead to concerns about staff communication and comfort, especially among part-time staff. The nature of teens and inconsistent participation and attendance in the space also presented challenges for management and gauging outcomes. Despite these challenges, the study showed the benefits of the spaces, pointing to gains in confidence, creativity, critical thinking skills, and innovation exhibited by youth participants.

YOUmedia has since been replicated in 12 of Chicago Public Library's branches, and there is a mobile program that allows staff at any branch to offer YOUmedia-based curriculum. Across the country, more than 30 learning labs have been created, comprising the YOUmedia Learning Labs Network. These labs focus on the same principles while taking local needs and barriers to inclusion into account (Sebring et al. 2013).

Previous chapters also discussed the benefits of including your teens in the program planning and presenting process. This is another fantastic way to take some of the burden off staff while engaging teens. Formulating a process that includes teens as active creators and managers of the process serves a dual purpose but pays ample rewards. Volunteers or mentors can also provide relief for staff. Understand that work in the early stages of the program to create a volunteer process and guidelines along with a teen engagement process will be valuable once the program is up and running. It is these processes that will allow you to transfer some of the burden from staff and ensure that the program is still running smoothly. If all goes correctly, the engagement processes themselves should do some of the connected learning work for you. Of course, this is another program element that you will want to evaluate and assess to ensure that it is working as expected.

WHEN AND HOW TO MAKE CHANGES: SMALL CHANGES OR BIG, PROGRAMMATIC CHANGES

Small changes often happen throughout the program, all along. It goes without saying that small changes can be harder to measure. These are the type of changes that you incorporate from one instance of offering the same program to the next: when you realize that your teens really need 30 minutes to do an activity, rather than 15, you note that offering a particular activity as a 2-hour program meant that you lost over half your audience in the last 30 minutes, or you note that a particular program was so popular that you really need extra staff or volunteers in the room. These are regular adaptations that we make to programs to ensure that they run as smoothly as possible the next time around. While this is an excellent practice, it does require some notation along the way. This ensures that you are properly documenting what worked best and when and where the program change occurred. Doing so ensures that anyone who follows the program after you will see the update and you can properly account for the improvement. Consider it the same practice as noting on a recipe when you make a modification that goes well. It is all in the interest of remembering and replication.

Evolving and Change in Connected Learning at Cuyahoga County Public Library

Before embarking on their transition to connected learning teen programming, the Cuyahoga County Public Library developed a set of outcomes to ensure that the program would achieve desired goals. Outcomes included the following:

- Young people use new media to grow academic achievement or future opportunity.
  - What I learned today will be useful to me in the future.
- Young people can easily access information to support self-directed and interest-driven learning.
  - I know how to discover more about this topic.
- Young people develop supportive and enriching relationships with caring adults and peers in a multifaceted learning environment.
  - I have connected with people who can help me learn more about this topic.
- Young people have a need to know and need to share.
  - I will continue to explore this topic on my own.
- I plan to show off what I've learned.
  - I will share projects that I create using my new skills.

Teens have been surveyed to gauge the effectiveness of the programs with the following survey questions:

- The adults here care about me.
- I feel comfortable going to an adult for help.
- I feel welcome here.
- Attending this program was worth my time.
- I learned or strengthened my knowledge or skills in this library program.
- I learned something that will be useful to me in the future.
- I know how to discover more about this topic after attending this program.
- I have connected with people who can help me learn more about this topic.
- I will continue to explore this topic on my own.
- I am able to share what I know with others in this program.
- I will plan to show off what I've learned.

Feedback during the rollout of the program to all branches has been positive but also showed that additional work to encourage deep dives into programs was necessary. The library will engage in additional work with staff to build comfort around making connections for teens and viewing themselves as educators. Additional work has also rolled out to ensure that mentors and volunteers are given an opportunity to talk about their professional choices and how the library's programs relate to the work that they do.

Large changes are best planned out and executed with sensitivity to timing and impact. Unless it is of an urgent nature for safety or security, too many changes or constant change will affect the stability and consistency of your program. Teens will become frustrated with the shifting ground and lose interest. As we explored in Chapter 7, attracting teens to programs can have its own challenges, and the less the library does to create an unpredictable environment, the better. With that in mind, large changes are often best executed at the beginning of a school year or semester. Differing schedules often change the makeup of your teen group at that time too and implementing structural changes to your program can accompany a fresh survey of teen interests and ideas. Sufficient notice about impending changes to programs, hours of service, and areas of interest supported are also essential. Teens, parents, administrators, and fellow staff will all appreciate ample notice about changes. Outcomes, assessments, and measurement tools must also be updated to ensure that changes in project design are reflected. Keep in mind that the way that you structure the changes and note them on your evaluation may affect your ability to track the outcomes of the program over the long term. Adding or removing questions from surveys complicates the process of exporting information to a spreadsheet and tracking data in columns. If you can avoid adding, modifying, or removing questions, that will help with data integrity. If you do have to add a question, consider doing it at the end to ensure that existing data is not disrupted.

SUMMARY

Assessments can be daunting, but they present the best opportunity to prove the value of your program. Following the below steps should help you construct a program that is built from the beginning with assessment in mind, allowing you to easily create or employ assessment tools to gauge the effectiveness of your outcomes.

- Develop and measure outcomes
- Determine the total cost of programs
- Include staff surveys and reflections
- Create and implement a plan for change

ACTION STEPS

1. If you have not already done so, develop a survey that measures the effectiveness of your program based on the outcomes you identified.
2. Consider tracking your program expenses as you go along. It makes providing the true cost of the program to your administration much easier. The spreadsheet included in Appendix B is a great way to do this.
3. If you have not already done so, consider engaging your teens and volunteers to take some of the program management off of staff.

Appendix A

Collection Development Resources

- **KIDMAP: The DIG Checklist for Inclusive, High-Quality Children's Media:** https://www.joinkidmap.org/digchecklist/. This is an evaluation rubric for educators, librarians, and parents to use when selecting digital media. The rubric was developed by Claudia Haines, youth services librarian and creator of "Evaluating Apps and New Media for Young Children: A Rubric."

Design Thinking Resources

- **Design Thinking for Libraries:** http://designthinkingforlibraries .com/. This is a toolkit designed specifically for librarians that provides an introduction to the design thinking process and how it can be applied to library work.

- **Design Thinking for Educators:** https://designthinkingforedu cators.com/. This is a toolkit designed for educators that provides an introduction to the design thinking process and how it can be applied to their work in the classroom.

- **Stanford d. school: A Virtual Crash Course in Design Thinking:** https://dschool.stanford.edu/resources-collections/a-virtual-crash-course-in-design-thinking. Learn the basic principles of design thinking while working through the steps of the Stanford d. school's virtual crash course. Access videos, handouts, and facilitation techniques for hosting or participating in a 90-minute design challenge.

Funding and Partnership Resources

- **YALSA Partnering to Increase Your Impact Toolkit:** http://www.ala.org/yalsa/sites/ala.org.yalsa/files/content/Partnerships_WebVersion.pdf. Information is available here on how libraries can identify, contact, and nurture partnerships. In addition to resources and information about partnerships, this toolkit contains sample communications that you can use when reaching out to potential partners.
- **Visualizing Funding for Libraries Data Tool:** http://libraries.foundationcenter.org/. This is a free data tool developed by the Foundation Center to help libraries and librarians identify funders.
- **Donors Choose:** https://www.donorschoose.org/. This is a crowdfunding platform created to support U.S. public schools. Teachers and librarians can create projects to support their classrooms and school libraries.

Making and Makerspace Resources

- **Making+Learning:** https://makingandlearning.squarespace.com/. This is a framework for libraries and museums new to making and makerspaces. Practitioners can find tools, resources, and guidance for developing their own makerspace. The Making+Learning project is a cooperative agreement between the Children's Museum of Pittsburg and the Institute of Museum and Library Services.
- **MakerEd:** http://makered.org/. This is a national nonprofit organization that supports maker-centered education by providing educators and organizations with tools and resources to create engaging learning experiences. The website includes a comprehensive resource library with program ideas and resources, professional development tools, and background research.
- **Make:** http://makezine.com/. An institution in the maker movement, Make: features DIY projects that encourage making and tinkering. Project categories include robotics, electronics, digital fabrication, crafting, and design.

- **YALSA Making in the Library Toolkit:** http://www.ala.org/
yalsa/making-library-toolkit. This toolkit was created by YALSA's
2014 Makerspace Resources Task Force as a resource for library
staff to integrate making into library programs and services.

- **Youth Makerspace Playbook by Maker Ed:** http://makered.org/
wp-content/uploads/2015/10/Youth-Makerspace-Playbook_
FINAL.pdf. This is a comprehensive guide to developing a youth
makerspace. The guide includes everything from space considerations to the types of tools and equipment to the educational
frameworks and learning approaches that can be used in a makerspace. There are also examples and links to youth makerspace
programs around the country.

Professional Development Resources

- **Edutopia:** https://www.edutopia.org/. This is an online community powered by the George Lucas Educational Fund with information, strategies, and resources for K-12 education.

- **Simple Interactions:** http://www.simpleinteractions.org/. This
is a professional development tool for youth work professionals
designed to encourage more high-quality interactions between
youth and adult facilitators in programs.

- **Teaching Channel:** https://www.teachingchannel.org/. Geared
toward classroom teachers, Teaching Channel is an online community where teachers can watch and share videos about educational
techniques and approaches and subject-specific lesson plans.

Programming Resources

- **DIY.org:** https://diy.org/. This is an online community for kids
aged 6–16 designed to drive and support a child's self-directed
learning and passion. The website also includes information for
educators who want to use DIY.org in a classroom or club.

- **Howtosmile:** https://www.howtosmile.org/. This is a free data-
base of educational math and science activities. You can search for
activities by topic, budget, or age of audience.

- **Instructables:** https://www.instructables.com/. Instructables is a
community where people can find and share instructions for projects and creations. From robots to home improvement projects to
food, you can find an instructable on just about anything.

- **Project Outcome:** https://www.projectoutcome.org/. This is a
free toolkit available to public libraries looking to use outcomes
to measure program effectiveness. Surveys are available for seven

library service areas: civic/community engagement, digital learning, economic development, education/lifelong learning, early childhood literacy, job skills, and summer reading. Project Outcome is managed by the Public Library Association.

- **YALSA STEAM Toolkit:** http://www.ala.org/yalsa/sites/ala.org.yalsa/files/content/YALSA_STEAMToolkit_WEB_Dec2016.pdf. This toolkit was created by a 2012–2013 YALSA task force as a resource for library staff on how to integrate STEAM (science, technology, engineering, arts, and math) into library programs and services. The toolkit was updated in 2016.

Research Resources

- **The Afterschool Alliance:** http://www.afterschoolalliance.org/. The Afterschool Alliance is a nonpartisan, national nonprofit focused on ensuring that all children have access to quality afterschool programs.
- **Connected Learning Alliance:** https://clalliance.org/. The Connected Learning Alliance includes resources and information about connected learning. The Connected Learning Alliance is managed by the Digital Media and Learning Research Hub.
- **The Digital Media and Learning Research Hub:** https://dmlhub.net. The Digital Media and Learning Research Hub conducts original research to investigate how digital media and technology is changing youth learning, participation, and culture. The Digital Media Learning and Research Hub is located at the University of California Humanities Research Institute and encompasses the Connected Learning Research Network and the MacArthur Research Network on Youth and Participatory Politics.
- **Educator Innovator:** http://educatorinnovator.org/. This is an online space for educators and organizations that are interested in the connected learning framework.
- **The Joan Ganz Cooney Center at Sesame Workshop:** http://www.joanganzcooneycenter.org/. This is an independent research and innovation lab that focuses on the impact of digital media on education and how new media can be used to help children learn.
- **P21 Partnership for 21st Century Learning:** http://www.p21.org/. P21 is a national nonprofit organization advocating for the importance of developing and creating 21st-century skills and learning opportunities for all students. The website includes information about P21's Framework for 21st Century Learning and resources for educators, parents, and policy makers.

Appendix B

FORMS

- Teen Program Survey
- Program Design Worksheet
- Program Cost Worksheet
- Sample Volunteer Job Description
- Sample New Volunteer Checklist
- Sample New Volunteer Orientation Outline

TEEN PROGRAM SURVEY

Do you have ideas about the programs you'd like to see at the library? Fill out this quick survey and let the teen librarian know what you want! Please return the completed form to the Information desk. Thanks for helping!

1. How do you find out about programs at the library?
2. Have you ever attended a library program for teens? If yes, what was it? If no, why not?
3. What kind of teen programs would you like to see at the library? (Check all that apply)
   - ❏ Anime/manga club
   - ❏ Coding
   - ❏ DIY programs
   - ❏ Entrepreneurship: Turn your ideas into a business
   - ❏ Gaming: Play games and learn to make your own
   - ❏ Robotics
   - ❏ Volunteer/community service projects
   - ❏ Writing clubs
   - ❏ Other (please specify) _____
4. What is the best time for you to come to a teen program at the library? (Check all that apply)
   - ❏ Weekday afternoons (until 5:00 pm)
   - ❏ What day(s): _____
   - ❏ Weekday evenings (after 6:00 pm)
   - ❏ What night(s): _____
   - ❏ Weekend afternoons
5. How often do you visit the library?
   - ❏ Every day
   - ❏ Several times a week
   - ❏ Once a week
   - ❏ Several times a month
   - ❏ Once a month
   - ❏ Rarely

6. What do you use the library for? (Check all that apply)
   - ❏ Hanging out with friends
   - ❏ Homework
   - ❏ Internet/computer use
   - ❏ Books to read for fun
   - ❏ Information for school
   - ❏ Programs/events
   - ❏ Other (please specify) _____

PROGRAM DESIGN WORKSHEET

Need	Goal/Outcome	Strategy	Ownership	Assessment
Describe the situation or problem	*Describe the desired result or conclusion of the situation*	*Describe how will you approach the problem including communications, funding, training, etc.*	*Describe who will be responsible for ensuring that the actions taken lead to the desired goal*	*Describe how you gauge if your strategies have been successful in the situation*

PROGRAM COST WORKSHEET

Date of Program		
Program Name		
	Cost	Notes
Staff Time	$	
Prep Time	$	
Outside Programmers	$	
Equipment	$	
Software or Apps	$	
Supplies	$	
Refreshments	$	
Marketing	$	
Totals	$	

SAMPLE VOLUNTEER JOB DESCRIPTION
Title: STEAM Connected Learning Volunteer

Purpose of the Position: This position will support teen librarians as they work to engage teens (ages 12–18) in connected learning activities. Projects may involve short- or longer-term volunteer commitments to help young people connect to a personal interest related to STEAM (science, technology, engineering, arts, and math).

Responsibilities:

- Engage with the teen to fully understand his or her STEAM interest
- Work with the teen librarian to help facilitate learning and to meet the objectives of the connected learning activities
- Encourage the teen to actively design the project and determine what research needs to be done to accomplish the project
- Facilitate learning activities
- Model and reinforce the learning in the project
- Collaborate with the teen librarian to ensure the teen can move forward with his or her project toward his or her desired goal
- Perform other duties as requested by the teen librarian

Position Requirements:

- Experience in one or more STEAM fields
- Willingness to work with teens aged 12–18
- Comfortable supporting the teen as he or she implements his or her connected learning project
- Willingness to coach and mentor teens in STEAM fields and help them see connections between their interests and potential education and/or career opportunities
- Commitment to staying with the teen until project is completed

Special Requirements:

Volunteers need to be excellent role models and communicators, be comfortable working with teens, and to demonstrate patience and concern for the teen's educational needs. Volunteer must guide and facilitate rather than complete the project for the teen.

Time Commitment: To be determined.

Training:

Volunteers will receive a general orientation from the volunteer coordinator and program-specific training from a teen librarian.

All volunteers will undergo a background check before being assigned to a branch or program. Any individual who poses a direct threat to the health and safety of himself or herself or others in the workplace will be deemed not qualified for this position.

SAMPLE NEW VOLUNTEER CHECKLIST

Name: _____

❏ Application Received
❏ Background Check

    ❏ Date Submitted: _____
    ❏ Date Processed: _____

❏ New Volunteer Orientation
❏ Begin Volunteering

SAMPLE NEW VOLUNTEER
ORIENTATION OUTLINE

While the specific information in volunteer orientations will look different from library to library depending on the goals of the volunteer program and the duties that the volunteers will perform, every orientation should include the following information:

- Welcome!
- Library mission statement
- Library code of conduct
- Volunteer program information
- Volunteer job description
- Recruitment process
- Application process
- Background check
- Volunteer scheduling
- Communication
- Closings due to unforeseen circumstances (e.g., weather emergency, power outage)
- Who does a volunteer contact about issues/problems?
- Questions?
- Thank the volunteers for donating their time!

REFERENCES

Afterschool Alliance. 2015. *Afterschool Programs: Inspiring Students with a Connected Learning Approach.* Washington, DC: Afterschool Alliance. http://after-schoolalliance.org/documents/Afterschool_and_Connected_Learning.pdf

Arzola, Rebecca, and Stefanie Havelka. 2015. "Mobile Apps in Collection Development: Supporting a Mobile Learning Environment." *The Charleston Advisor,* 16 (3): 43–45.

Braun, Linda W., Maureen L. Hartman, Sandra Hughes-Hassell, and Kafi Kumasi. 2014. *The Future of Library Services for and with Teens: A Call to Action.* Chicago: Young Adult Library Services Association. http://www.ala.org/yaforum/sites/ala.org.yaforum/files/content/YALSA_nationalforum_Final_web_0.pdf

Bruce, Mary, and John Bridgeland. 2014. *The Mentoring Effect: Young People's Perspectives on the Outcomes and Availability of Mentoring.* Washington, DC: Civic Enterprises with Hart Research Associates for MENTOR: The National Mentoring Partnership.

Center for Promise. 2015. *Don't Quit On Me: What Young People Who Left School Say about the Power of Relationships.* Washington, DC: America's Promise Alliance.

COSI. 2000. "Simple Machines." COSI/Columbus. http://cosi.org/downloads/activities/simplemachines/sm1.html

Fontichiario, Kristen. 2014. "Interview with Leslie Preddy, author of School Makerspace, 6-12." *MakerBridge*, March 10, 2014. http://makerbridge.si.umich.edu/2014/03/interview-with-leslie-preddy-author-of-school-library-makerspaces-6-12/

Gallup, Inc. 2016. *Gallup Student Poll U.S. Overall Fall 2016 Scorecard.* http://www
  .gallupstudentpoll.com/197492/2016-national-scorecard.aspx

Goleman, Daniel. 1998. "What Makes a Leader?" *Harvard Business Review,*
  November–December 1998.

Haines, Claudia. 2017. Interview by the authors. Phone Interview. Parma, OH,
  November 17, 2017.

Horrigan, John B. 2016. *Digital Readiness Gaps.* Pew Research Center. http://www
  .pewinternet.org/2016/09/20/digital-readiness-gaps/

Ito, Mizuko, Kris Gutiérrez, Sonia Livingtone, Bill Penuel, Jean Rhodes, Katie
  Salen, Juliet Schor, Julian Sefton-Green, and S. Craig Watkins. 2013. *Connected Learning: An Agenda for Research and Design.* Irvine, CA: Digital Media
  and Learning Research Hub.

Kaner, Sam. 2014. *Facilitator's Guide to Participatory Decision-Making.* San Francisco:
  Jossey-Bass.

Kepple, Sarah. 2013. "Intentionally Backwards, the Future of Learning in Libraries." *Young Adult Library Services,* 12 (1): 33–37.

Lenhart, Amanda, Maeve Duggan, Andrew Perrin, Renee Stepler, Lee Rainie, and
  Kim Parker. 2015. *Teens, Social Media & Technology Overview 2015: Smart-
  phones Facilitate Shifts in Communication Landscape for Teens.* Pew Research
  Center. http://www.pewinternet.org/2015/04/09/teens-social-media-tech
  nology-2015/

Martin, Crystle. 2016. "A Library's Role in Digital Equity." *Young Adult Library
  Services,* 14 (4): 34–36.

McNair, Kate. Spring 2016. "Creating a Culture of Learning at Your Library." *Young
  Adult Library Services,* 14 (3): 27–31.

The Mentoring Center. 2017. http://mentor.org/

Mirra, Nicole. 2017. "Connected Learning to Connected Teaching." *Educatorinno-
  vator.org,* August 1, 2017. http://educatorinnovator.org/from-connected-
  learning-to-connected-teaching-a-necessary-step-forward/

Nashville Public Library Foundation. 2017. http://nplf.org/

National Assessment of Educational Progress. 2014. Technology and Engineering Literacy (TEL) Assessment. https://www.nationsreportcard.gov/
  tel_2014/files/TEL_101_infographic.pdf

Potter, Ned. 2013. "Marketing Libraries is like Marketing Mayonnaise." *Library
  Journal,* April 18, 2013. http://lj.libraryjournal.com/2013/04/opinion/
  advocates-corner/marketing-libraries-is-like-marketing-mayonnaise/#_

Potter, Ned. 2012. "Marketing Your Library." *American Libraries,* November
  13, 2012. https://americanlibrariesmagazine.org/2012/11/13/marketing-
  your-library/

Putnam, Robert D. 2015. *Our Kids: The American Dream in Crisis.* New York:
  Simon & Schuster.

Rhodes, Jean E. 2017. "The Future of Youth Mentoring." *DML Central Digital Media
  + Learning: The Power of Participation,* June 12, 2017. https://dmlcentral.net/
  future-youth-mentoring/

Rideout, Victoria, and Vikki S. Katz. 2016. *Opportunity for All? Technology and Learning in Lower-Income Families.* New York: The Joan Ganz Cooney Center at
  Sesame Workshop. http://www.joanganzcooneycenter.org/wp-content/
  uploads/2016/01/jgcc_opportunityforall.pdf

Search Institute. 1997, 2006. *40 Developmental Assets for Adolescents.* Minneapolis, MN: Search Institute. http://www.search-institute.org/content/40-developmental-assets-adolescents-ages-12-18

Sebring, Penny Bender, Eric R. Brown, Kate M. Julian, Stacy B. Ehrlich, Susan E. Sporte, Erin Bradley, and Lisa Meyer. 2013. *Teens Digital Media and the Chicago Public Library.* Chicago: The University of Chicago Consortium on Chicago School Research. https://consortium.uchicago.edu/sites/default/files/publications/YOUmedia%20Report%20-%20Final.pdf

Skokie Public Library. 2017. Skokie Public Library BOOMbox. https://skokielibrary.info/blog/boombox/

StatCounter Global Stats. 2016. "Mobile and tablet internet usage exceeds desktop for first time worldwide." News Release, November 1, 2016. http://gs.statcounter.com/press/mobile-and-tablet-internet-usage-exceeds-desktop-for-first-time-worldwide

Subramaniam, Mega. 2016. "Designing the Library of the Future for and with Teens: Librarians as the 'Connector' in Connected Learning." *The Journal of Research on Libraries & Young Adults* 7: n.p. http://www.yalsa.ala.org/jrlya/wp-content/uploads/2011/02/Subramaniam_Designing-the-Library_Final.pdf

Trouern-Trend, Katherine, Audrey Sumser, Kathy Mahoney, Caroline Aversano, Samantha Marker, and Kimberly Bolan Cullin. 2012. *National Teen Space Guidelines.* Chicago: Young Adult Library Services Association. http://www.ala.org/yalsa/sites/ala.org.yalsa/files/content/guidelines/guidelines/teenspaces.pdf

Tyler, Ralph W. 2013. *Basic Principles of Curriculum and Instruction.* Chicago: University of Chicago Press.

Wikipedia. 2017. "Backwards Design." https://en.wikipedia.org/wiki/Backward_design

Yorio, Kara. 2016. "North Jersey Makerspaces combine hands-on creativity with STEAM Subjects." *NorthJersey.com,* February 24, 2016. http://www.northjersey.com/story/life/community/2016/02/24/north-jersey-makerspaces-combine-handson-creativity-with-steam-subjects/94509564/

BIBLIOGRAPHY

Abbas, June, and Kyungwon Koh. 2015. "Future of Library and Museum Services Supporting Teen Learning: Perceptions of Professionals in Learning Labs and Makerspaces." *The Journal of Research on Libraries & Young Adults* 6. http://www.yalsa.ala.org/jrlya/wp-content/uploads/2011/02/Subramaniam_Designing-the-Library_Final.pdf

American Association of Higher Education. 2012. *Principles of Good Practice for Assessing Student Learning.* National Institute of Learning Outcomes Assessment. http://www.learningoutcomeassessment.org/PrinciplesofAssessment.html

Arzola, Rebecca, and Stefanie Havelka. 2016. "Apps in Higher Education: Criteria and Evaluation." *The Charleston Advisor* 17 (3): 55–57.

Bartz, Laurie. 2016. "Community Experts Mentor Teens and New Adults." *Young Adult Library Services* 14 (2): 18–19.

Bass, Hayden, Kelly Czarnecki, Angela Frederick, Rachel McDonals, Matthew McLain, and Sara Ryan. 2015. *Teen Programming Guidelines.* Chicago: Young Adult Library Services Association. http://www.ala.org/yalsa/sites/ala.org.yalsa/files/content/TeenProgramingGuidelines_2015_FINAL.pdf

Bohn, Rachael, Derrick Burton, Markita Dawson, Billie Moffett, Dina Schuldner, Bill Stea, and Adrienne Strock. 2017. *Partnering to Increase Your Impact.* Chicago: Young Adult Library Services Association. http://www.ala.org/yalsa/sites/ala.org.yalsa/files/content/Partnerships_WebVersion.pdf

Braun, Linda, Sarah Park Dahlen, Valerie Davis, Maureen Hartman, Sandra Hughes-Hassell, Vanessa Irwin, Crystle Martin, Lynda Salem-Poling, and Erin Wyatt. 2017. *Teen Services Competencies for Library Staff.* Chicago: Young Adult Library Services Association.

Charles, Cassidy. 2012. "Can I Check This Out?: Circulating Collections beyond Books, CDs, and DVDs." *Public Libraries Online*, November 15, 2012. http://publiclibrariesonline.org/2012/11/can-i-check-this-out-circulating-collections-beyond-books-cds-and-dvds/

Chen, Milton. 2013. "The Rise of *Any Time, Any Place, Any Path, Any Pace* Learning: Afterschool and Summer as the New American Frontier for Innovative Learning." In *Expanding Minds and Opportunities: Leveraging the Power of Afterschool and Summer Learning for Student Success*, edited by Terry K. Peterson, 107–109. Washington, D.C.: Collaborative Communications Group, Inc.

Dowds, Ally, Catherine Halpin, and Jess Snow. 2017. "Teen Leadership Development Through a Teen Gaming Program." *Young Adult Library Services* 15 (4): 33–38.

Dudley, Michael Q. 2013. *Public Libraries and Resilient Cities*. Chicago: ALA Editions.

Falk, John H., and Lynn D. Dierking. 2010. "The 95 Percent Solution: School Is Not Where Most Americans Learn Most of Their Science." *American Scientist* 98, 486–493.

Farrelly, Michael Garrett. 2012. *Make Room for Teens: A Guide to Developing Teen Spaces in Libraries*. Santa Barbara, CA: Libraries Unlimited.

Fink, Megan P. 2015. *Teen Services 101: A Practical Guide for Busy Library Staff*. Chicago: American Library Association.

Garcia, Antero, ed. 2014. *Teaching in the Connected Learning Classroom*. Irvine, CA: Digital Media and Learning Research Hub.

Gardner, Howard. 2015. "The Good Citizen in a Digital Era." *Huffington Post*, December 3, 2015. http://www.huffingtonpost.com/howard-gardner/the-good-citizen-in-the-d_b_8703174.html

Gibrich, Christie. 2015. "Libraries Are for Making: Making Connections That Is." *Young Adult Library Services* 13 (2): 27–29.

Herr-Stephenson, Becky, Diana Rhoten, Dan Perkel, and Christo Sims. 2011. *Digital Media and Technology in Afterschool Programs, Librarians, and Museums*. Cambridge, MA: MIT Press.

Hoffman, Kelly M, Mega Subramaniam, Saba Kawas, Ligaya Scaff, and Katie Davis. 2016. *Connected Libraries: Surveying the Current Landscape and Charting a Path to the Future*. College Park, MD: The ConnectedLib Project.

Hopwood, Jennifer. 2014. "How Not to Reinvent the STEM Wheel: Using Crowdsourcing and Community Partners." In *How to STEM: Science, Technology, Engineering, and Math in Libraries*, edited by Vera Gubnitskaia and Carol Smallwood, 171–178. Lanham, MD: Scarecrow Press.

Horrigan, John B. 2015. *Libraries at the Crossroads*. Pew Research Center. http://www.pewinternet.org/2015/09/15/libraries-at-the-crossroads/

Horrigan, John B. 2016. *Libraries 2016*. Pew Research Center. http://www.pewinternet.org/2016/09/09/2016/Libraries-2016/

Ito, Mimi. 2017. "It's the Relationships, Stupid: Connected Camps Mid-Summer Report." DML Central Digital Media + Learning: The Power of Participation, July 27, 2017. https://dmlcentral.net/connected-camps-mid-summer-report/

Ito, Mimi. 2017. "5 Secrets to Creating an Innovative After-school Program." DML Central Digital Media + Learning: The Power of Participation, September 27, 2017. https://dmlcentral.net/5-secrets-creating-innovative-school-program/

Ito, Mizuko, Sonja Baumer, Matteo Bittanti, danah boyd, Rachel Cody, Becky Herr-Stephenson, Heather A. Horst, et al. 2010. *Hanging Out, Messing Around, and Geeking Out: Kids Living and Learning with New Media*. Cambridge, MA: MIT Press.

Jacobson, Mikael. 2016. "Going Inside the Box the Wired Library." Public Libraries Online, November 28, 2016. http://publiclibrariesonline.org/2016/11/going-inside-the-box-the-wired-library/

Koester, Amy. 2015. "Welcome to the BOOMbox, Skokie's STEAM Space." The Show Me Librarian, January 12, 2015. http://showmelibrarian.blogspot.com/2015/01/welcome-to-boombox-skokies-steam-space.html

Lankes, R. David. 2015. "Expect More: Why Libraries Cannot Become STEM Educators." Paper presented at the Public Libraries and STEM: A National Conference on Current Trends and Future Directions, Denver, Colorado, August 20–22, 2015. http://www.nc4il.org/images/papers/Lankes_Expect%20More.pdf

Lankes, R. David. 2016. *The New Librarianship Field Guide*. Cambridge, MA: MIT Press.

Martin, Crystle. 2015. "Connected Learning, Librarians, and Connecting Youth Interest." *The Journal of Research on Libraries & Young Adults* 6. http://www.yalsa.ala.org/jrlya/2015/03/connected-learning-librarians-and-connecting-youth-interest/

Palfrey, John. "Connected Learning Now." *Independent School*. Summer 2013. https://www.nais.org/magazine/independent-school/summer-2013/connected-learning-now/

Pandora, Cherie P., and Stacey Hayman. 2013. *Better Serving Teens through School Library–Public Library Collaborations*. Santa Barbara, CA: Libraries Unlimited.

Pattee, Amy. 2014. "Rethinking Library Collections for Young Adults." *Young Adult Library Services* 12 (3): 15–17.

Paul, Annie Murphy. 2015. "How to Ensure that Making Leads to Learning." *School Library Journal*, May 12, 2015. http://www.slj.com/2015/05/research/how-to-ensure-that-making-leads-to-learning/#_

Preddy, Leslie. 2016. "Sneak Peak: The Power of Makerspaces." *School Library Connection*, October 4, 2016. https://blog.schoollibraryconnection.com/2016/10/04/sneak-peek-the-power-of-makerspaces-with-leslie-preddy/

Rainie, Lee, and Janna Anderson. 2017. The Future of Jobs and Jobs Training. Pew Research Center. http://www.pewinternet.org/2017/05/03/the-future-of-jobs-and-jobs-training/

Reardon, Sean F. 2011. "The Widening Academic Achievement Gap between the Rich and the Poor: New Evidence and Possible Explanations." In *Wither Opportunity? Rising Inequality, Schools, and Children's Life Chances*, edited by Greg J. Duncan and Richard J. Murnane, 91–115. New York: Russell Sage Foundation.

Seelye, Katharine Q. 2014. "Breaking Out of the Library Mold, in Boston and Beyond." *The New York Times*, March 7, 2014. https://www.nytimes.com/2014/03/08/us/breaking-out-of-the-library-mold-in-boston-and-beyond.html

Sefton-Green, Julian. 2013. *Learning at Not-School: A Review of Study, Theory, and Advocacy for Education in Non-Formal Settings*. Cambridge, MA: MIT Press.

Stephens, Wendy. 2014. "Checking Out Tomorrow's School Library Collections."
    Young Adult Library Services 12 (3): 18–20.
Stout, Rachel. 2015. "Hand in Hand: Teens, Tech, and Community Engagement."
    Young Adult Library Services 13 (2): 21–24.
Velásquez, Jennifer. 2015. *Real-World Teen Services*. Chicago: ALA Editions.

INDEX

ABOUT THE AUTHORS

MEGAN E. BARRETT is information and technology literacy specialist for the Cuyahoga County Public Library. When she isn't working with iPads, 3D printers, or robots, Megan works closely with staff to create and facilitate programs that foster connected learning in their branches. A former teen librarian, Megan is a youth advocate committed to creating opportunities to engage and empower teens. She has a master's in library and information science.

REBECCA J. RANALLO is information and technology literacy manager for the Cuyahoga County Public Library, where she oversees innovation, implementation, and training. In an environment where technology is constantly changing, she works to help staff embrace the challenges and recognize the value to our community of integrating technology in the library. She has a master's in library and information science and a background in adult technology instruction.